War Photography

War
Photography

EDITED by THOMAS BARFIELD

Magpie, London

Constable & Robinson Ltd
3 The Lanchesters
162 Fulham Palace Road
London W6 9ER

This edition published by Magpie Books,
an imprint of Constable & Robinson Ltd 2005
www.constablerobinson.com

Designed by
Katherine Winterson, Spokes Design

ISBN 1 84529 270 7

Printed and bound in China

1 3 5 7 9 10 8 6 4 2

Contents

THE ROLES AND USES OF WAR PHOTOGRAPHY

War, like a lot of things, had already been photographed by the time the French poet Charles Baudelaire launched an impassioned attack on photography as a whole in the Revue Française in 1859. It may have been only 20 years old, but it already had ideas way above its station. Some 'mad fools' actually thought it was an art form. It was high time, Baudelaire thundered, that photography 'return to its true duty, which is to be the servant of the sciences and the arts – but the very humble servant, like printing or shorthand, which have neither created nor supplemented literature. Let it hasten to enrich the tourist's album and restore to his eye the precision which his memory may lack; let it adorn the naturalist's library, and enlarge microscopic animals; let it even provide information to corroborate the astronomer's hypothesis; in short, let it be the secretary and clerk of whoever needs an absolute factual exactitude in his profession – up to that point nothing could be better.'

Photography has, of course, resolutely refused to remain in its place ever since (and, ironically enough, Baudelaire would have wholeheartedly approved of many of the artistic applications it has subsequently given itself to). It has had an oddly circular history, proving to be, by turns, the most experimental and the most mainstream of any artistic medium. It has developed an uncanny gift for affecting people in ways that are both instantly familiar and spectacularly new, whilst at the same time never shedding its aura as a child of science, the servant, as Baudelaire put it, of whoever needs 'absolute factual exactitude'. It has retained a mantle of scientific proof; the expectation that what is photographed will always accurately transcribe reality, that the camera will never lie. Hence, the extraordinary, longstanding relationship photography has had with war. For war is pre-eminently a place where truth – the truth of who is alive or dead, of who is winning or losing, of what acts are being committed - is at a premium.

It was General Dwight Eisenhower, the Supreme Allied Commander in World War Two, who said that 'fundamentally, public opinion wins wars.' Public opinion is, of course, the preserve of journalism, and all its branches have been of comparable influence in shaping the perception of a war – one only has to think of the renown of war journalists such as Ernest Hemingway and Ryszard Kapuscinski, or TV reporters like John Simpson or Rageh Omah. But photography has a conspicuously central role. It is uncanny to think that, even in this age of satellite phones, live video feeds and 24 hour news channels, some of the most influential visual images from the Second Gulf War and its aftermath have been photographs – the pictures of the torture of Iraqi prisoners in Abu Ghraib prison by 372nd Military Police Company, and of the American civilian contractors killed in Falluja by insurgents and hung from the bridge.

One wonders, although of course it is impossible to tell, whether they will come to symbolise the war in the way that such iconic, infamous images as those of the American photographer Eddie Adams and the Vietnamese photographer Hung Cong 'Nick' Ut became symbols of the Vietnam War. Adams's is a sequence of pictures, in which a prisoner, supposedly a Vietcong lieutenant, is led to the Vietnamese chief of police, Brigadier General Nguyen Ngoc Loan, who without warning pulls out a pistol and shoots him dead. Ut's, on the other hand, is a single image. The South Vietnamese air force has inadvertently dropped napalm on a village, and four children are running towards the camera, one of them, the nine-year old Kim Phuc, naked and screaming, 'Too hot, please help me.' Such pictures capture something so brutally powerful, and do so in such a haunting, expressive way, that their force does not diminish at all over time – the opposite, in fact: they become the memory and narrative of the whole war.

Photographs are powerful things, and all war photography reflects, to varying degrees, the policies adopted by governments and militaries to control their nature and the flow of information as a whole. President Bush's ban on photographs of soldiers' coffins returning home from the Second Gulf War is no different to President Roosevelt's ban on photographs of American dead in the Second World War, which was only lifted in September 1943. Some wars, such as the First World War and First Gulf War, have been so tightly censored that they have yielded only a very partial visual record. Others, most famously the Vietnam War, have been field days for photographers; everything was laid on for them, even airfares, as if the war were a vast spectacle for which the military were hoping to get good reviews. The Second Gulf War, meanwhile, tried to find a third way, with the practice of 'embedding' allowing journalists unprecedented access to the frontline, although it is a moot point at what cost. But whatever the approach, the overall war effort has always been the reason given. Censorship has been construed as protecting strategic information and, by extension, public morale; openness has been a weapon in the battle for hearts and minds.

How much this has clashed with journalism's concern for accurate information and impartial reporting of events from both sides has varied from war to war. In the First and Second World Wars, reporters were in uniform and perfectly happy to think of their job as an extension of the war effort. They frequently chafed under the yoke of censorship, since they felt that there was so much more they could show, as it happened, rather than months later. In the Second World War, for instance, they only really had freedom to document events with any immediacy after D-Day and the turning of the tide in Europe. But, broadly speaking, journalists and military felt they were engaged in the same task and waging a just war.

In what became a paradigm of wars of oppression of all stripes, the Spanish Civil War, photographers such as the Jewish Hungarian Robert Capa, who has good claim to be the presiding genius of war photography, showed what dedicated and brilliant partisan photographers could do for a cause. Capa produced one of the most famous images of tragic heroism, a Republican militiamen at the moment of death, arcing backwards, arm and rifle outstretched, on a scrubby, helpless hillside. He also, in the face of the widespread atrocities committed against civilians – the bombing of Guernica, the columns of refugees – arraigned war itself. The spirit of Goya entered his work. He put himself in the face of great danger because he wanted to share everything, bear witness to every suffering, every instance of fortitude, defiance and optimism. As John Steinbeck said of Capa, 'He knew that you cannot photograph war, because it is largely an emotion. But he did photograph that emotion by shooting beside it. He could show the horror of a whole people in the face of a child. His camera caught and held emotion. His pictures are not accidents. The emotion in them did not come by chance. He could photograph motion and gaiety and heartbreak. He could photograph thought. Capa's work is itself the picture of a great heart and an overwhelming compassion.'

Every war photographer hopes the war they are photographing will be the last. After the First World War a book of war photographs was published entitled War Against War. W. Eugene Smith, one of the leading photographers for the American magazine, Life, said 'I hoped that my photographs might be not the coverage of a news event, but an indictment of war – the brutal corrupting viciousness of its doings to the minds and bodies of men – and that my photographs might be a powerful emotional catalyst to the reasoning which would help this vile and stupid criminality from beginning again.' These fervent hopes crystallized into a passionate and pioneering determination to illuminate the realities of war when, almost without pause, the world settled into the Second World War and the conflicts of the Cold War and post-colonial civil strife.

The Korean War was subjected to the same military censorship as the Second World War, but Vietnam became a proving ground for a particular sort of intimate, immediate war photography, in which photographers constantly exposed themselves to greater dangers in their search to make the viewer feel as if they were there with the soldiers or civilians. Naturally each photographer's work reflected his politics – David Douglas Duncan, a marine who believed US intervention in Vietnam was correct and refused to accept the authenticity of Ronald L Haeberle's My Lai photos, long after they had irrefutably been proven authentic, showed the heroic, epic side of war. Courage, comradeship, stoicism are the hallmarks of his pictures of soldiers on their tours of duty.

Philip Jones Griffiths, by contrast, said in retrospect, 'I always thought that soldiers running up and down hills firing at each other was the most boring aspect of what actually happened in Vietnam. What was really important was the efforts by one society to subjugate another society and the resistance of the subjugated.' Many photographers, covering CIA-sponsored coups against leftist Latin American governments, or civil wars in Third World countries that resulted from colonial dispositions but were then largely ignored in

First World countries, shared this view of war as injustice, strong oppressing weak. They were their country's conscience, gadflies, the bearers of truths no one wanted to hear. As Jones Griffiths put it, 'To me, there is no point pressing the shutter unless you are making some caustic comment on the incongruities of life. That is what photography is all about. It is the only reason for doing it.'

War, however, is notoriously resistant to simple definitions. In 1978, Jorge Lewinski could write in The Camera at War, 'In any case the nature of war has been totally transformed. It is no longer a matter of personal sacrifice for a cause. There seems to be no cause big enough or important enough to draw men together. Modern war is not so much a flexing of individual muscle; it is the probability of total annihilation.' Then came 9/11. No one could doubt that huge numbers of the military in Afghanistan and Iraq saw themselves as determined to sacrifice their all for a cause. The debate was less whether there could be such a thing as a just war as whether there could be such a thing as a 'war on terror', where war, however 'clean' and 'smart' was understood in a conventional sense. Was this really the way to respond to terrorism?

But meanwhile something else had happened to perceptions of war, namely information overload and the triumph of the mass media. Suddenly there were images of wars from all over the world competing for exposure in newspapers and magazines, and the criteria by which they were selected seemed to have less to do with any universal values of justice than with scale – was a world power involved or was world peace threatened – and impact – were they preternaturally shocking, brutal or sensational? In the 1860s Baudelaire had deplored the fact that, 'Every newspaper, from the first line to the last, is nothing but a tissue of horrors. Wars, crimes, thefts, lecheries, tortures, the evil deeds of princes, of nations, of private individuals; an orgy of universal atrocity. And it is with this loathsome appetizer that civilized man daily washes down his morning repast.' Now, apart from a mounting wave of celebrity trivia, there was the added confusion that while a newspaper's motives may have been commercial, its rhetoric was that of humanitarian sympathy which had become so dominant in the 1960s. The unspoken justification for showing images, even if they were just there to sell papers, was always that if people see things, they, or the situation, will improve. People will protest or lobby or fundraise or promote other means of conflict resolution.

Like all the credos of the 1960s, it wasn't long before this credo was challenged. People claimed that there was no proof of the humanist principle that knowledge is virtue, that if someone knows something they will do the right thing. He may do nothing, or it may even numb him and make him less likely to act in general. Nor are the photographers necessarily such untainted paragons. They may have many different motives for their work and ambiguous attitudes to war. They may be attracted as well as repelled by war, fired by the same sorts of ambition as the soldier without wishing to incur the guilt of killing. Photographs can seem more and more enigmatic. As Diane Arbus said, 'A photograph is a secret about a secret. The more it tells you, the less you know.'

Ours is a much more media-critical age, and we subject images to a much harsher scrutiny. We also sense a palpable, constant urge among the media to push back the boundaries of what it is permissible to show, an ever-greater incursion of violent, brutal, sadistic material into our lives. Suddenly this has been rendered completely incomprehensible by horrifying propaganda material that seems atavistic and yet somehow intended as a modern advertisement for a cause. One senses that the horrendous videos of beheadings of hostages by Iraqi insurgents in the aftermath of the Second Gulf War will continue to be profoundly shocking and troubling for a long time.

No doubt we entertain as many illusions about ourselves as any other generation, whilst deluding ourselves that we are the most hard-headed. But I think a consensus now would hold that a primary requirement of a war photograph is that it be a good photograph. This is no Wildean, art-for art's sake statement. It is simply to say that a photograph can still have an extremely powerful effect, but exploitative, voyeuristic images and saturation of the market means that the standards are very high. The second point on which people could agree I think is that, while it is harder for war photographers to claim any higher purpose for themselves – peace campaigners, freedom fighters and so on – they can with great pride acknowledge their mission to document and record what war is and what it does. The Polish poet Zbigniew Herbert put this with poignant subtlety in his poem, Report from the Besieged City, 'They graciously gave me the inferior role of chronicler. I record I don't know for whom the history of the siege... all of this is monotonous I know it can't move anyone.' The poet adopts a humble, self-deprecating persona, and yet as the poem continues, as the siege approaches its foregone conclusion, it becomes apparent how vital and noble his role is; 'cemeteries grow larger, the number of defenders is smaller yet the defence continues it will continue to the end and if the city falls yet a single man escapes he will carry the city within himself on the roads of exile. He will be the City.' The innate values inherent in all art are a key component of war photography, which, in a sense, is the Perseus of the art forms. It has to work out how to capture the Medusa of warfare without either the photographer or the viewer being turned to stone. Another challenge it faces, of course, is that it is unbelievably dangerous.

'If your pictures aren't good enough, you're not close enough,' was Robert Capa's favourite dictum, and to understand war photography, one has to, on the one hand, have a sense of the technical developments that allowed people over time to get ever closer to the action, and on the other, a sense of those people who grabbed that hair-raising opportunity.

Roger Fenton, the first photographer officially to record a war, arrived in the Crimea in 1855 with a horse-drawn darkroom – a converted wine merchant's van – 2 assistants, 5 cameras, 36 cases of equipment, 700 glass plates and 3 horses from Gibraltar. The wet-collodion process he used had been introduced 5 years previously and was a great improvement over daguerrotypes and calotypes. Exposure times had been cut from minutes to seconds, the definition and tonal quality were excellent and the negatives could be easily printed. The one drawback, however, was that the plate had to be both exposed and developed while wet. Hence, Fenton's panoply of accoutrements. Not only did Fenton not travel light, but he had to photograph at dawn to prevent the developing baths boiling in the intense heat, whilst steering clear of the Russian batteries, to which his van presented an inviting target. He stayed for three months and, having contracted cholera, returned to find himself so famous that he was allowed to lie down during an interview with Queen Victoria. His photographs had utterly changed the public mood.

When England and France launched an invasion force of 57,000 troops into the Crimea in September 1854 to counter the Russians' incursion into the Ottoman Empire, it was one of the largest military enterprises ever undertaken. Within months, however, poor organisation, lack of equipment, disease and exposure had wrought havoc in the allied ranks. The Light Brigade charged to their deaths, Inkerman was lost, the Times was filled with devastating reports by their correspondent William Russell and Lord Aberdeen's government resigned in 1855. There was an urgent need of good news. One photographic unit was killed when its ship went down with all hands in a hurricane. The next couldn't master the technical difficulties of photographing in such difficult conditions. Finally Fenton, a well-known artistic, landscape and portrait photographer, volunteered and produced as comforting, in the main, a series of photographs as the government could have desired. His tableaux may have occasionally had titles such as 'Hardships of Camp Life', but this only emphasised, by contrast, their soothing content – well-fed men, plentiful supplies, good provision for the wounded. Altogether characteristic is a picture called, 'His Day's Work Over', featuring Lieutenant Colonel Hallewell leaning back as a servant fills his glass.

Only one picture rises above the requirements of propaganda, an uncanny landscape entitled the Valley of the Shadow of Death, which shows a Crimean valley littered with Russian cannonballs. This image has entered the iconography of war as a hauntingly unforgettable scene, whilst at the same time representing an early example of the practice of staging and manipulating photos. For Fenton not only took a picture of what he found, he also had his assistants rearrange the cannonballs in more aesthetic ways. In this he anticipates the First World War photographs of men going over the top, which were taken on training grounds, or Joe Rosenthal's famous image of the Stars and Stripes being raised after the capture of Iwo Jima from the Japanese in World War II. This in fact was the second flag that had been raised on the island. Staff Sergeant Louis R. Lowery had been filming the first being raised in the morning when hand grenades thrown by a hidden Japanese soldier nearly killed him and blew up the flag. Later the same day the ceremony was repeated with a larger flag and a more careful composition. This was the photo that Yevgeny Khaldei of the Soviet news agency TASS saw and then copied during the fall of Berlin. He found a Soviet flag and sent soldiers up to the Reichstag roof to raise it. Photographs, as everyone well knows, and yet somehow can forget – such is their insistency and aura of perceived truthfulness – are very easy to stage.

The American Civil War was heavily photographed by a team of photographers marshalled by Matthew Brady, an Irish photographer of whom Abraham Lincoln said, 'Brady and the Cooper Union Speech made me President.' Brady claimed credit for many of the most famous pictures, such as of the Gettysburg battlefield, which in fact were taken by assistants such as Timothy O'Sullivan and Alexander Gardner. In September 1862, he put on an exhibition called 'The Dead of Antietam' in New York. 'The dead of the battle-field come up to us very rarely, even in dreams,' wrote a reporter for The New York Times. 'We see the list in the morning paper at breakfast, but dismiss its recollection with the coffee. There is a confused mass of names, but they are all strangers; we forget the horrible significance that dwells amid the jumble of type...We recognize the battle-field as a reality, but it stands as a remote one. It is like a funeral next door. It attracts your attention, but it does not enlist your sympathy. But it is very different when the hearse stops at your front door and the corpse is carried over your own threshold...Mr. Brady has done something to bring to us the terrible reality and earnestness of the War. If he has not brought bodies and laid them in our door-yards and along [our] streets, he has done something very like it.'

All the photographs were static shots – the cameras were not yet able to capture movement – and a prominent role of photographers in that conflict was to set up temporary studios at the military encampments. There they made and sold tintype or carte portraits of the soldiers, who then sent them home and waited for their families to send equivalent portraits back to them. This humblest, talismanic function of photography – Look! I'm still alive! – is still central to a camera's role in war. One only has to look at the website flickr, which is used for sharing photos over the web, to see that most are very simple portraits by soldiers of other soldiers. They're alive, the days are passing, they'll be home soon. These photos function like votive objects.

In the 1890s, faster films, better lenses, hand cameras – Kodak – and the growth of commercial developing and printing services led to a huge growth in photography. Lots more people did it, and took photos of lots more subjects. But a long time was to pass before this was reflected in war photography. On the outbreak of the First World War, the British government invoked the new Official Secrets Act and Defence of the Realm Act and sought to ban all war reporting. This was later commuted to a handful of war correspondents in uniform, working under a pool system for publication in the national press, heavily controlled by army escort officers and intensive censorship. Individual soldiers were forbidden to carry cameras, and military photographers taking pictures for intelligence and reconnaissance had to display great technical ingenuity and courage. Lieutenant OGS Crawford of the Royal Engineers, whose camera was once destroyed by a sniper, explained that taking pictures of the battlefield was 'a lengthy business, involving anything up to a dozen or more exposures of several seconds each, between which the plate has to be changed. The camera revolved on a graded tripod... I had several narrow shaves.' Basil Clarke, reporting for War Illustrated, gave what might be a blueprint for a universal, romantic identikit of what a war photographer should be, 'War photography either creates or attracts to itself an especial breed of men – men who are either so engrossed in their craft, or so constituted mentally and physically that the riskiness of their work has very little effect on them – and is certainly no deterrent... Of this type of camera man a good example is Lieutenant Brooks... Brooks has no nerves at all. Ruddy-cheeked, and with twinkling, boyish eyes, he seems to go through his work with as little concern as a boy. he has generally an example of the latest thing in German hand-grenades in his pocket, which he shows and handles with most disquieting sang-froid, and day after day he goes poking his camera's nose into places which any normal man, left free to roam in the war zone as Brooks is, would shun by as many miles as possible.'

Unfortunately Brooks and his colleagues were unable to do everything they were capable of and, although there are many good photos from the First World War, in a way the most telling are those taken from planes, such as the devastating pairing of photos of Passchendaele's battlefield before and after the fighting between June and December 1917. The human scale, the intimacy and pathos of the individual soldier and civilian would have to wait for later.

The heyday of photojournalism began in 1925 when the Leica camera came on the market. Picked up by photographers attracted by its unobtrusiveness and speed, its grainy, ultra-close and animated photographs were in turn championed by the illustrated magazines that began in Germany and France, and when the Nazis came to power, migrated west to England and America. Picture Post, Life, Colliers, Vu and many others were the platform for two or even more generations of great war photographers – the Magnum Photo Agency's founding generation – Capa, Henri Cartier Bresson, David 'Chim' Seymour, George Rodger, Margaret Bourke White, Lee

Miller, Bert Hardy, Carl Mydans – and the generation that followed – Larry Burrows, Philip Jones Griffiths, Raymond Depardon, Don McCullin, Catherine Leroy and many more. They took many wonderful pictures, and many died trying to do so. 135 photographers died or disappeared while covering the wars in Indochina. George Rodger swore never to cover a war again after photographing Belsen. Without thinking, he found himself working out shots through his viewfinder, arranging the emaciated skeletons into formal compositions; it shocked him to his core. The age-old conundrum for the photographer of what to do, when to stop photographing, is it all just exploitative, gave him no peace. Capa landed on Omaha Beach with the second wave of American troops. He took 134 photographs with two cameras and then managed to get back to England. The lab technician in London used too much heat developing the pictures and destroyed all but 11, which went on to become the basis for the opening sequence of Steven Spielberg's Saving Private Ryan. The lab technician, Larry Burrows, himself went on to be, not in a movie, but one of the most famous photographers of the Vietnam War, known as 'the compassionate photographer' by Marines. He was killed when his helicopter was shot down in 1971.

Photojournalism's golden era probably ended in the 1980s, when the magazines that ran the pictures started to focus on celebrities and escapism, and the advertising revenue that paid for them migrated to television. The Falklands War saw a return to old-fashioned military censorship, whilst the fall of communism ushered in a new chapter in European conflict. Reacting tragically late, Nato's intervention in Kosovo introduced the notion of a humanitarian war mainly conducted from the air. The technological aspects of this – 'smart' bombs, computer battlefield mapping, precision targeting – furnished an image of a 'clean' 21st Century war that in the First

Gulf War, after Saddam Hussein had invaded Kuwait in 1991, was reinforced by very tightly controlled news management. In Desert Storm, reporters were based in Saudi Arabia and subjected to a pool system which kept them well away from the battlefield and the front lines, restricted to daily briefings for their news. When they could, photographers were as brave and revealing as ever. Only one photographer, Bill Biggart, died when the World Trade Centre in New York was destroyed by al-Qaeda in 2001. But he, like all the photographers there, took amazing pictures before he did so.

The US's first response, Operation Enduring Freedom, which overthrew the Taliban regime in Afghanistan, again revolved around a deep suspicion for the press. The US military sought to create the impression of an antiseptic war without extraneous casualties or damage. Coverage was initially limited to night images of explosions over Kabul, a fascination with the weapons and military aircraft used, aerial 'before' and 'after' images intended to confirm 'surgical' strikes. Depleted uranium, civilian casualties, friendly fire were all incredibly sensitive issues; journalists at an American marine base were on one occasion locked in a warehouse to keep them from reporting on US troops hit by friendly fire. According to Jon Swain of the Sunday Times, a huge al-Qaeda ammunition cache 'discovered' in the mountains and blown up in front of massed TV cameras was in fact a 'friendly' arms dump belonging to local warlord who was an ally of American-backed provisional government in Kabul. It was only a matter of time, however, before reports began appearing of children's deaths and atrocities committed by Northern Alliance soldiers.

In the face of sustained media protest against such restrictive news management, the Pentagon promised more access for certain reporters who would be 'embedded' in individual military units. 'Embedding means living, eating, moving in combat with the unit you're attached to,' said Pentagon spokesman Bryan Whitman. Like the First World War, reporters would be in uniform. They could chose to leave their units for any reason, 'But once you do that, there are no guarantees that you'll get another opportunity with that unit or necessarily even with another unit. That's what I'm talking about when I say [a reporter] embeds for life.' The practice has proved as controversial as the war itself. Although there has been a wealth of imagery and reporting from the frontline, there has been a worry that it lacks context or impartiality. John Simpson of the BBC declared, 'I didn't want to be part of it because I didn't want to dependent on the people I was reporting on for my security, my food, my transport. We need to have independent journalists moving around.' He was also convinced that the Americans and British only allowed it because they were convinced the war would be a 'walkover'. That, of course, is one of the great mysteries of the Second Gulf War. In one way, it was over so quickly – only 21 days to the fall of Baghdad – and yet in another, under the guise of insurgency, it has gone on so long, and military tactics that initially seemed unimpeachable appear, since the reprisals in Falluja that well-nigh decimated the town, questionable. Photo stories keep on coming in from embedded photographers, many of very high quality, but it is the wildcards, the uncontrollable images like those of Abu Ghraib, that show how central a part photography still plays in war.

Robert Capa said that every war photographer's most fervent wish is unemployment. There is no sign of that ever happening, but this book shows the manifold accomplishments and insights war photographers will vouchsafe us while mankind continues to indulge in this bloody, brutal and agonising practice.

by Giles H. Wynn

PART ONE

THE BREAK-UP OF THE OLD ORDER

Balkan conflicts – the First World War –
the decline of old empires – the rise of modern
warfare – consequences of the peace

An Italian officer leads a column of Arab prisoners, Turco–Italian War, 1911–12

During the Turco–Italian War of 1911–12, Italian officers lead a column of soldiers escorting Arab prisoners. The lead officer holds a captured Turkish flag. The year-long war was a significant step towards the First World War. Italy aimed to capture North African provinces including Tripolitania and Cyrenaica in Libya as well as the Dodecanese archipelago and the Greek island of Rhodes from the Ottoman Empire. The Italians gained significant provinces in October 1912 after the Turks signed a peace treaty. The newly awakened nationalism in Italy would become a significant factor in the two World Wars.

The war also demonstrated the vulnerability of the Ottoman Empire, which strengthened nationalism in subject provinces such as the Arab nationalism that would play a strong part in the First World War. The first significant use of aircraft in battle came in the Turco–Italian War. An Italian aeroplane was used early in the war to spy on enemy lines, and the first bomb dropped from an aeroplane in combat fell on Turkish troops in Libya in 1912. In these ways the war prefigured the far more deadly warfare that was to follow.

Turkish cavalry, Constantinople, 1912

Countries in the Balkans were encouraged in their local territorial ambitions by the perceived weakness of the Ottoman Empire in the Turco–Italian War. The Young Turk Revolution of 1908 had led to progressive changes in the Ottoman Empire in previous years. Montenegro and Bulgaria had become independent kingdoms, Serbia had aspirations to Kosovo and land to the south, while Greece wanted to expand its territory to areas such as Crete and Thessaloniki. While Turkey was still fighting Italy in Libya, the 'Balkan League of Christian States' – Greece, Serbia, Bulgaria and Montenegro – demanded immediate autonomy for another of Turkey's territories, Macedonia, and, on receiving what it considered an unsatisfactory response (anything short of Turkey getting out of Europe entirely would have been unsatisfactory) declared war. Supplied with German arms and advised by German officers, the Turkish army mobilised in force in October 1912 for what became known as the First Balkan War. These cavalry are members of the First Army detailed to protect Constantinople.

Bulgarian artillery, First Balkan War, 1912

Bulgarians firing from a hill position during the First Balkan War in 1912. Bulgaria had only been independent by this stage for thirty-four years, but within fourteen days of mobilization, it fielded an army of 400,000 men – out of a population of five million. Over the next four weeks, it moved the army over 160 miles into Turkish territory, captured one fortress – Adrianople – and invested another, won two battles and reached the gates of Constantinople.

Balkan War, 1912

A Turkish refugee walking in the mire of the high road to Constantinople behind his caravan, during the retreat by Turkish forces from the combined Serbian and Bulgarian armies during the Balkan War of 1912. Turkey suffered devastating casualties – twelve infantry divisions out of a starting total of forty-three – and lost more than four fifths of its European territory and over two thirds of the population of its European provinces. At the Treaty of London in 1913, it was only allowed to keep Constantinople and a narrow strip of land to the west of it. Germany's prestige suffered – the rout was a slight on its arms and military advice – and the Serbs' victory was a setback to Austrian imperialism.

Serbian women in training

Thwarted by the Austrian annexation of Bosnia and Herzegovina in 1908, Serbian nationalism inspired the First and Second Balkan Wars. After the assassination of Archduke Franz-Ferdinand in Sarajevo, Austria blamed Serbia for inciting violence and declared war on 28 July 1914. Within five days, Russia, Germany, France and Britain were also at war. The Serb army won the first Allied victory on 19 August, defeating the Austrians at Sabac, but Serbia's civilian population bore the brunt of the nation's casualties. 650,000 Serb civilians died during the First World War. Here Serbian women are instructed in how to use rifles after the declaration of war.

Volunteers queue to enlist, Britain, 1914

Volunteers queue to enlist outside a British recruiting office in 1914. The First World War has justifiably been called 'the most popular war in history'. People flocked from all over the British Empire to join up – over 2.5 million, a fair number of whom were underage – and apart from the professional soldiers of the British Expeditionary Force who crossed to France in August 1914, the British army was largely a volunteer one until conscription was introduced in January 1916. For most British, a matter of honour was at stake – upholding the treaty with Belgium which guaranteed Britain's protection from invaders – and the war itself was expected to be a brief one – 'a brisk, merry war', as the Germans put it.

In August 1914, the Order of the White Feather was founded by Admiral Charles Fitzgerald. The organization encouraged young women to give out white feathers to men who had not enlisted. The government became concerned about the number of state employees leaving to join up and the Home Secretary was even asked to have members of the Order arrested for 'conduct likely to disrupt the police'. He refused, although employees were issued with badges that stated they were serving King and Country. In the atmosphere of public hysteria, many men joined up even in the absence of conscription.

British troops sleeping, Boulogne

The British High Command banned soldiers from using cameras – they could be shot if found doing so – and the few official photographers – two army officers were eventually permitted to cover the entire Western Front – were subjected to tight censorship. All photographs were pooled, the majority suppressed – a process of which the photographers themselves wholly approved. Death was often just alluded to, as in this picture of British soldiers sleeping on the quay of Boulogne harbour. Classical art frequently referred to the kinship between sleep and death. As Ovid asked, 'What's sleep but death's cold reflection?'

'Hotel de Ritz', France

After the Western Front became deadlocked as two opposing sets of trenches that stretched for almost 25,000 miles, from the British Channel to the Swiss Frontier, the Ritz for frontline soldiers was generally a trench six-feet deep and three-feet wide, a muddy cesspool rife with rats and lice, where canned beef, 'bully', constituted the highlight of the British menu. The trenches bred their own diseases – trench fever and trench foot, from standing in mud and water – and spawned a life of filth, danger and tedium. The patriotic press and military obviously wanted to sanitise it all, but the soldiers themselves were often equally willing to pretend that all was well. They were worried lest they might be seen as barbaric if the true circumstances of the war were revealed. At the same time, in trench journals such as The Wipers Times, they wanted to mitigate the conditions of the war by ridiculing and exaggerating them.

Scottish troops practising a bayonet charge

Scottish soldiers practising a bayonet charge. Like its cavalry counterpart, the infantry charge was seen as the paradigm of martial valour, and the bayonet the infantry weapon sans pareil. In fact the opportunities to use it in trench warfare were very limited. Infantry advancing with fixed bayonets were invariably mown down by machine guns before they reached enemy trenches. Even when a raiding party had reached the enemy position the role of the bayonet was often primarily one of guarding the grenadiers among their party, who would race down the trench lobbing hand grenades into dugouts as they passed. The French nicknamed the bayonet la fourchette (the fork) and le cure-dents (the tooth pick).

British troops charging from a trench

A photograph of British troops charging from a trench which, while it may not actually be one of the many posed in Britain, seems to represent an idealized vision of 'going over the top'. The trenches were generally deeper, entangled with barbed wire, and subjected to unrelenting barrages of artillery, quite apart from the snipers who lay in wait to pick off anyone who raised their heads above the parapet. The troops were generally given rum before they went over, and for a long time 'shellshock', which would paralyse soldiers at the bottom of the ladder, was taken for cowardice and sufferers would be shot.

Troops praying, 1914

Troops on their knees praying during a religious service in late 1914 on the battlefield. This regiment lost half their men in a battle the previous month and, at that stage, the casualty lists were still published in daily newspapers. The practice was soon discontinued because so many of the volunteer regiments came from the same village or town, and so many were killed that towns would suddenly lose half their populations. Publication of casualties stopped, and reinforcements were drawn from all over Britain rather than from the same place. At a relatively early stage of the war, one can already see the indelible mark of experience in the faces of individual soldiers.

Australian stretcher-bearers, the Dardanelles

Winston Churchill was not the only influential figure to believe that an eastern breakthrough would help to break the stalemate that had been reached with fighting on the Western Front. Other leading figures in England and France agreed with his theory that this could be the way forward. The strategic importance of the Dardanelles Straits was that by capturing them, the allies would have a direct route to Constantinople, by which they might put Turkey out of the war, and a direct supply route to Russia.

Initial attempts to take the Straits with purely naval force (Churchill's preferred option) in early 1915 failed, forcing the allies to consider a ground invasion, which many believed would secure the peninsula. The ground offensive was to be undertaken by a force of 75,000, made up predominantly of untested Australian and New Zealand troops, who would go on to suffer terrible losses in the fighting. Troop landings in April secured small beachheads but failed to make any progress. Further landings in subsequent months made no more headway, but cost many lives. Even so, reinforcements were sent and the massive landings at Suvla Bay and elsewhere were launched in August 1915.

Confidence at home in the whole operation ebbed. British First Sea Lord Admiral Fisher dramatically resigned on 15 May 1915 over Churchill's handling of the Dardanelles campaign and as a result Churchill too resigned, his political career apparently in ruins. Events elsewhere intruded as the invasion of Serbia made further troop reinforcements unlikely. Meanwhile a significant body of men was trapped fighting on a narrow strip of exposed land, dug into dangerous trenches, with shortages of supplies and a paralysis of leadership. To this day Australians, while proud of the bravery of their troops in the Dardanelles and elsewhere, remember Gallipolli as one of the most terrible chapters of their history, and one in which the British leaders let them down in the most disastrous fashion.

Evacuation, Gallipoli

To compound the errors of the Dardanelles campaign, British commanders dithered about whether or not to order an evacuation. Ian Hamilton, Commander-in-Chief of the campaign was reluctant to evacuate, but was removed from his post, and replaced by Sir Charles Monro. Monro recommended evacuation in October, but Kitchener would not sanction this until he had personally seen the conditions – after further political manoeuvring, the evacuation was finally ordered in early December.

By now, heavy snow had fallen, making the operation more difficult, and conditions on the ground even worse. In spite of this a successful evacuation was organised – 105,000 men and 300 guns were moved from Anzac Cove and Suvla Bay over the course of ten days, with a minimum of casualties. A variety of stratagems were used to prevent the Turks from realizing that this was a full evacuation until late in the process, thereby improving the safety of the operation. The nearby Helles contingent was evacuated by early January and the Dardanelles experiment was finally over.

Churchill later wrote of Monro 'he came, he saw, he capitulated'. Unable to accept that the project had been a mistake from the start, he blamed the man who had at least managed to mitigate the disaster by getting the remaining troops out alive. The picture shows Australian troops tending to wounded comrades on the Gallipolli peninsula during the evacuation.

British troops giving German prisoner a drink, 1916

British troops giving German prisoner a drink on the Western Front in 1916. For the most part, the opposing sides were entrenched a few hundred metres apart, firmly separated by no-man's-land. But occasional meetings between the two sides, such as here after the German soldier has surrendered, could affirm that they had more in common than their leaders led them to believe. One of the most remarkable events of the war was the Christmas truce in 1914 when ordinary soldiers from both sides met in no-man's-land to exchange presents and even to play football, before returning to fire from their trenches on Boxing Day.

British plane dropping torpedo

A Royal Flying Corps aircraft drops a torpedo towards its target. The idea for a military air force had only come about in 1911 after Prime Minister Asquith asked the Committee for Imperial Defence to examine the possibilities for creating an air force. Other countries including France, Germany and the USA were at this point at a more advanced stage of preparation for aerial military action. The first bomb-dropping experiments soon followed and in July 1914, only a month before the outbreak of war, a Short seaplane became the first British plane to drop a torpedo.

For the early stages of the war, the French air force undertook a heavier work load than the British because it was at a more advanced stage, but technological advances and aggressive leadership meant that the Royal Flying Corps played a stronger role by 1916, a year in which over 700 flyers died in combat.

Canadian troops on tank

From a nation of only seven million, 600,000 Canadians fought on the allied side in the First World War, of whom 60,000 died. The battle-hardened Canadian Corps fought the battles that captured Hill 70 and Vimy Ridge in 1917. The Canadian commander Lieutenant-General Sir Arthur Currie, who had led the assault on Hill 70, was asked to send his troops in to capture Passchendaele, following two previous battles for the village. He questioned the orders, stating that the objective might be achieved but at a likely cost of 16,000 men. The terrain for the battle was terrible, a sea of mud that had been churned up by successive battles and constant bombardment, and Passchendaele has become a byword for the horrors of the war. The allied commander Haig, by now used to high casualty levels, overrode Currie's doubts, and the Canadian Corps eventually captured Passchendaele, ending the battle, at a cost of 15,000 dead or injured out of 20,000 men.

New Zealand soldiers in a trench, 1916

Soldiers from New Zealand, having consolidated their position in the trenches, rest and enjoy bread and jam in September 1916. Over 100,000 soldiers from New Zealand fought in the First World War.

French troops charging

French soldiers charge across a field with rifles raised, an image that recalls the warfare of the nineteenth century. No one had known what sort of conflict the First World War would be, nor how the world would be transformed by it — which is not to say, of course, that many people didn't feel they knew. Helmuth von Moltke, Germany's Chief of Staff, for instance, declared that the war he and his predecessor, Alfred von Schlieffen, were planning 'would destroy the culture of all Europe for decades to come.' But such chilling bravado only emphasized the profound and widespread ignorance of the war's nature and consequences.

Moltke clearly didn't anticipate that his personal failure to give clear orders at the Battle of the Marne in September 1914 would halt the hitherto lightning advance of German troops and precipitate the stalemate and hell of four years of trench warfare — his last act as Chief of Staff. But more generally, neither Moltke nor his fellow strategists had any inkling that the twentieth century progress, the technological, scientific and institutional developments in which they put their faith — the accelerated transport and supply lines, the improved communications, the vastly more powerful firearms and artillery, the better medical provisions — would have hideously paradoxical effects. Rather than securing the famous 'victory by Christmas', the breakthroughs of the industrialized age would actually benefit defence rather than offence, creating a type of 'total' war that was at once uniquely destructive and uniquely difficult to win.

The aerial bomber, the U-boat, poison gas and, above all, high explosives mechanized the business of killing, rendering it impersonal, unpredictable and incomparably more devastating than anything before. Trains reaching speeds of up to 100 mph hurried troops to the battlefield, but once the men left the railheads they had to march like a Napoleonic army. The size of the continental armies — at least three million strong, sometimes six — made it harder for either side to score decisive victories, while supply lines could keep the men under arms, fed and free from lethal epidemics — in uniquely miserable conditions — almost indefinitely. Meanwhile the generals launched frontal attack after attack, refusing to accept the dominance of defensive capabilities.

Entrenched troops, the Somme

Shrapnel bursting over a reserve trench in the Canadian line in mid-October of the Somme campaign. The battle began on 1 July 1916, on which day at least 20,000 British soldiers were killed and a further 40,000 were injured. It is the greatest number of British casualties in a single day's fighting in modern history. The battle continued until November and was a defining moment of the conflict.

Only the Crimean and Franco–Prussian Wars had threatened the peace of Europe for much of the nineteenth century, which meant that generations of men with no experience of combat were only too eager to rush to defend King, or Emperor, and country. War was still invested with a chivalric and ennobling glamour, and armies were subjected to ruthless censorship and propaganda. It was a number of years before Horace's saying: Dulce et decorum est pro patria mori (It is sweet and fitting to die for one's country) became, in Wilfred Owen's words, an 'an old lie told to children ardent for some desperate glory'.

Nine million people died and twenty-one million were wounded in the Great War. The Austro-Hungarian and Ottoman Empires fell; the Romanov, Habsburg and Hohenzollern dynasties came to an end. The Bolsheviks rose to power, and communism became the first mass ideology of the twentieth century, soon to be followed by liberal democracy and fascism. Europe ceased to be the counterweight of the world, the financial centre of gravity shifted to New York, Japanese expansionism emerged in East Asia, anti-colonial movements sprung up from West Africa to Indonesia, and ethnic and religious divisions were exacerbated around the globe.

The social effects were almost as momentous. In wartime economies, industrialized labour, trade unions, and socialist parties gained in power, while some landed interests declined. The mass employment of women led to the transformation of their social and political position, despite predictable resistance. Women received the vote in eleven countries between 1915 (Denmark) and 1920 (USA). Everything was thrown into question by the Great War – a cultural crisis swept through the arts, religion, literature, lifestyles – and there are times, even now, when the shadows cast by it seem to grow ever longer, darker and more daunting with each passing year.

Scottish sentry, Salonika, 1915

Scottish sentry guarding stores in the Greek port of Salonika. Anglo-French forces began landing at Salonika on 5 October 1915, with the intention of providing assistance to the Serbs who were under attack from combined German, Austro-Hungarian and Bulgarian armies. They were too late – weakened by typhus, over 200,000 Serb soldiers and civilians fled over the mountains into Albania, and from there were evacuated by sea to Corfu. Rather than withdrawing, however, as the British advised, the Allies then set about fortifying Salonika.

Serbian trooops, Salonika, 1917

The 1st Regiment of the Serbian Army at Salonika in 1917. Reinforcements arrived in Salonika throughout 1916 and the campaign to retake Serbia claimed the fall of Monastir in November 1916. They had to wait almost two years for their next success: a Serbian victory west of the River Vardar led to Bulgaria's surrender on 30 September 1918. It was a brutal and neglected campaign, plagued by malaria. The British forces suffered 162,517 cases of the disease and in total 505,024 non-battle casualties.

The wreckage of a German Gotha aircraft, 1917

British troops guard the wreckage of a German Gotha in a French field, 1917. Developed in the autumn of 1916 to supersede the Zeppelin, the Gotha twin-engined bomber had a wingspan of over seventy-seven feet (twenty-three metres), a range of 800 km (500 miles) and a bomb load of up to 500 kg (1,100 lb). Based in Belgium, their first sortie against Britain was a twenty-one plane raid on Folkestone which killed ninety-five people. In mid-June, a fleet of eighteen Gothas attacked London in daylight, killing 162, and, although they were countered by over ninety British fighters, did not suffer a single loss. For the next four weeks they raided London almost daily until the light and manouevrable Sopwith Camel was given a greater defensive role; from then on, the unwieldy Gothas could only fly at night. In total, 835 were killed and 1,990 wounded by their raids.

A downed German hydroplane

A German hydroplane disguised in American colours which was shot down by Americans in the Mediterranean. The First World War began only just over a decade after the Wright brothers' first twelve-second flight, but it saw a prodigious increase in the role and capabilities of the aeroplane in war. It was used for observation, reconnaissance, tactical and strategic bombing on sea as well as land. 'Seaplane tenders' were long considered the most practical; ships carrying a small number of seaplanes that could be lowered by crane over the side and then winched back on deck at the end of their flight. But in the autumn of 1918 the British navy launched the first true aircraft carrier, the HMS Argus. Orville Wright wrote to a friend that, 'The aeroplane has made war so terrible that I do not believe any country will again care to start a war'.

German troops with flamethrower, 1917

German troops attacking with a flamethrower in 1917. Flamethrowers were first used by the Germans in a surprise attack on the British at Hooge in Flanders in 1915, with devastating results. The shock and the concentrated power of the German models – the smaller one had a range of eighteen metres, the larger thirty-six, with flames lasting for forty seconds – initially proved very effective at clearing trenches. As time went on, however, the British and French developed their own models and Flammenwerfer duty became extremely hazardous. Not only would the small groups – generally of four to six men, with two operating a flamethrower between them – be the target of sustained fire, but the machines often blew up themselves.

French troops at Mont de Signes, 1917

French troops taking the last crest at Mont des Singes, part of the Chemin des Dames ridge, a four-kilometre stretch of the Hindenburg Line which constituted their sole success in the Second Battle of the Aisne. Plans for the disastrous Nivelle Offensive, named after its architect, the French Commander-in-Chief Robert Nivelle, were discovered by the Germans, who had plenty of time to dig in. On the first day, 16 April 1917, the French lost 40,000 men alone, and 187,000 in all before the offensive was called off on 9 May. The French Army subsequently mutinied and Marshal Petain could only restore order by telling the British that they would have to shoulder the main burden on the Western Front until American forces arrived.

American troops in France, 1918

American troops on the move in France in 1918. On 2 April 1917, US President Wilson signed a declaration taking America into the war. He had run for re-election in 1916 on the ticket, 'he kept us out of war', and during the 976 days of US neutrality, had repeatedly tried to negotiate a peace settlement. But public indignation at the Zimmermann telegram – a telegram from the German Foreign Secretary to the German Ambassador in Mexico suggesting a German/Mexican alliance against the United States – and the resumption of German submarine attacks on American civilian shipping forced his hand. The American Expeditionary Force, commanded by General Pershing, reached significant strength in the summer of 1918, and substantially boosted Allied morale and capability.

The crossing of the St Quentin canal, 1918

Soldiers of the South Stafford and North Stafford Regiments after crossing the St Quentin Canal – part of the Hindenburg Line – in 1918. This was a very formidable obstacle. The canal was thirty-five feet wide, with wire in the water and eight feet of mud, two bridges defended with wire and machine gun posts, and a continuous line of trenches on the precipitous rise above the canal. The night before the attack, a bombardment was fired by 1,044 field guns and howitzers and 593 medium heavy guns and howitzers; mustard gas, high explosives and shrapnel were used. Although expected, this was effective, and the Staffordshires crossed the canal using rafts and lifelines and stormed the bridges before they could be blown up. In an hour and forty minutes they captured a position that would have kept them pinned down for months in 1916 and 1917.

Wounded soldiers

British and French wounded heading back to their lines, presumably discharged from one of the casualty clearing stations – the mobile hospitals close to front line which were intended to allow soldiers to be operated on before sepsis and gangrene set in. Such images of blinded men leading one another in single file by the hand, often after being caught by gas shells without their masks, became iconic representations of the First World War. The pathos of the suffering and the sense of solidarity between the men gave these photographs a particular charge.

Canadian stretcher bearers, 1918

Men of the Canadian Medical Corps with a wounded soldier on a stretcher in 1918. Gas masks at the start of the war were notoriously rudimentary – the wearer often couldn't inhale – but by 1918, filter respirators using charcoal or antidote chemicals were standard issue. Although Germany was arguably the most avid proponent of the use of poison gas (it was constantly researching new forms – chlorine, phosgene, mustard gas) all the powers used it, and there were over a million casualties from gas during the war. The suffering was especially cruel. The effects of mustard gas, for instance, came on twelve hours later – massive blistering, internal and external, nausea, vomiting, build up of mucus fluid on lungs, and such pain that victims generally had to be strapped to their beds. Death took up to four or five weeks.

Canadian artilleryman with Belgian baby

A Canadian artillery man tries to amuse a Belgian baby after his mother was killed, and the child was wounded, by German artillery. After the invasion of Belgium in 1914, stories of German atrocities against the Belgian civilian population became such a staple of Allied propaganda that it was hard to tell how true they were. But the chief of the general staff, Helmuth von Moltke, freely admitted to deploying 'extraordinarily harsh' measures against civilians, in part in reprisal against Belgian snipers, or franc-tireurs (literally, 'free-shooters'), operating behind German lines. Independent Belgium during the war consisted solely of a small strip of coast between Ypres and the French border, including Nieupoort, to where the Belgian king moved his court. Over a quarter of a million Belgian refugees fled to Britain.

German battleships being escorted to Scapa Flow by a US battleship, 1918

German battleships being escorted to Scapa Flow by a US battleship in 1918. After the armistice, seventy-four ships of the German High Seas Fleet were ordered into Scapa Flow, a natural harbour used as the northern base of the British Grand Fleet. They arrived in November 1918, and stayed there for 10 months, during which time, unsurprisingly, they became a popular tourist attraction. One could hire boats to go out to see them. When Rear Admiral von Reuter, the German Officer in command at Scapa Flow, realized in June 1919 that Germany would have to accept Allied peace terms, he decided it was impossible for the fleet to surrender and waited for the bulk of the British Fleet to leave the Flow for exercises before ordering a final, dramatic act of resistance.

German battleships being scuttled at Scapa Flow, 1919

On 21 June 1919, Rear Admiral von Reuter gave the order for the German fleet to be scuttled. The first ship, the Friedrich der Grosse – the flagship of the Jutland Fleet – went down at 12.16 pm; the last, the Hindenberg, at 5 pm. Onlookers were stunned by the extreme gesture – not least because the ships were manned with full crews who had to struggle for their lives – and the British only managed to save a few of the German ships by towing them towards shore. Salvage began soon afterwards, and only eight German ships now lie on the seabed.

Sinn Féin volunteers drill with dummy rifles, 1916

Sinn Féin, meaning 'ourselves' or 'we ourselves', was a party established by Arthur Griffith in 1905. It was one of the Irish republican movements which swelled its ranks in the wake of the suspension of the Home Rule Bill and which took part in the Easter Uprising.

The General Post Office in Dublin in ruins, 4 May 1916

Dubliners walk through the remains of the General Post Office in Sackville Street (now O'Connell Street) in Dublin following the Easter Rebellion against British rule. The uprising took place on Easter Monday, 24 April 1916, and was centred on Dublin. Its chief objective was the attainment of political freedom and the establishment of an Irish republic – republicans were frustrated at the suspension of the Home Rule Bill as a result of the First World War. Padraic Pearse, James Connolly and their companions became heroes for their defiance in raising two flags – the golden harp on a field of green and the Irish tricolour – from the roof of the General Post Office and declaring independence from Britain. The rising was eventually put down after a Royal Navy gunboat had been shelling the GPO for some time. There were many casualties: 794 civilians and 521 police and troops killed or wounded. Realizing that further resistance was futile, Pearse surrendered unconditionally. Fifteen of the group of rebels, including Pearse, Connolly and Thomas McDonagh were sentenced to death and executed by firing squad in Kilmainham Jail. Four others, including American-born Eamon de Valera, were sentenced to death, though the sentences were later commuted to life imprisonment. In fact, de Valera and some others were granted amnesty the next year. Another leader of the rebellion, Sir Roger David Casement, the British consular agent, was convicted of treason and hanged. Many others received long prison sentences.

Rebel prisoners being marched out of Dublin, 1916

Suspension of the Home Rule Bill had stimulated the growth of the Citizen Army, an illegal force of Dublin citizens organized by labour leader Jim Larkin and the socialist James Connolly; of the Irish Volunteers, a national defence body; and of Sinn Féin. The leaders of these organizations planned the uprising which began at midday on 24 April 1916 when 2,000 men led by Padraic Pearse seized the General Post Office in Dublin and other strategic points in the city. Shortly afterwards the rebels declared the independence of Ireland and the establishment of a provisional government. By the following morning they occupied a significant part of Dublin. Martial law was declared and British reinforcements gradually reclaimed rebel positions. By 29 April the rebels had surrendered. The following are the names of all the rebels executed by the British in the aftermath of the rebellion: Padraic Pearse, Thomas McDonagh, Thomas Clarke, Joseph Plunkett, Edward Daly, Michael O'Hanrahan, William Pearse, Sean McBride, Con Colbert, Eamonn Ceannt, Michael Mallin, Sean Hueston, James Connolly, Sean McDermott, Roger Casement and Thomas Kent.

Funeral for the dead of the Tsarskoye Selo Revolution, Russia, 1917

Russian soldiers and workers listen to loudspeakers at the graveside of those who fell during the Tsarskoye Selo Revolution. The dead were buried in the grounds of the ex-Tsar's palace. On the evening of 12 November 1917 Cossacks under Kerensky launched a counter-revolutionary assault on the town. They were repulsed by concerted fire from the sailors, Red Guards and soldiers manning barricades. Armoured cars of the revolutionary forces pursued them as they retreated and Kerensky's arrest was ordered. Tsakskoye Selo was taken by revolutionary troops.

Russian Battalion of Death women, 1917

On 7 November 1917, the provisional government of Russia was overthrown by the Bolsheviks bringing Lenin and Trotsky to power. Lenin signed a peace treaty with Germany, pulling Russia out of the First World War. However the newly formed Red Army was immediately engaged in fighting the Whites, supporters of Tsar Nicholas II. The Battalion of Death was one of several female battalions on both sides. It was stipulated that in order to be allowed to fight at the front they had to shave their heads.

The final journey of the Unknown Soldier, France, November 1920

The honour guard for the funeral of the Unknown Soldier drawn up outside the chateau near Boulogne where the coffin was kept overnight before the journey back to Britain for burial in Westminster Abbey. In 1916, the Reverend David Railton, while serving as a military chaplain in France had noticed a rough wooden cross on which was inscribed 'An Unknown British Soldier'. He had later written to the Dean of Westminster who subsequently became the leading force in the construction of the Tomb of the Unknown Soldier. The remains of four unknown British war casualties were exhumed from Aisne, the Somme, Arras and Ypres and taken to St Pol in the north of France in November 1920 where they were laid in a chapel, each one under a Union Flag. Brigadier General L. J. Wyatt, commander of all British troops in France and Flanders selected one of the unknown soldiers at random and two officers placed the body in a plain coffin and sealed it; the remaining three bodies were reinterred at a nearby military cemetery. The following morning a service was held to commemorate the sacrifice of the Unknown Soldier and the body was then escorted under a French honour guard to Boulogne, drawn by a wagon with six horses and followed by a mile-long procession. On 9 November the plain coffin was placed inside another constructed of oak from Hampton Court secured with bands which incorporated a sixteenth century crusader's sword from the Tower of London's collection. HMS Verdun, escorted by six warships, carried the coffin of the Unknown Soldier to Dover where its arrival was greeted by a nineteen-gun salute. Six warrant officers from the four services carried the coffin to be taken by train to Victoria Station in London. On Remembrance Day, 11 November 1920, six black horses drew the coffin through crowd-lined streets. The carriage halted outside Whitehall where King George V unveiled the Cenotaph. The King, his three sons, members of the Royal Family and government ministers then followed the coffin through the streets to Westminster Abbey. The Unknown Soldier was laid to rest having passed through an honour guard made up of 100 British and Canadian recipients of the Victoria Cross. King George V sprinkled soil from the battlefield at Ypres – six barrels of Ypres earth had accompanied the Unknown Soldier home to England so that his coffin might lie on the soil where so many of his comrades had lost their lives. For seven days the tomb was watched over by a guard of honour while thousands of mourners passed by to pay their respects. On 18 November a temporary stone – it was later replaced with black Belgian marble – with the following inscription sealed the tomb: 'A British Warrior Who Fell in the Great War 1914–1918 for King and Country. Greater Love Hath No Man Than This'.

PART TWO

CIVIL STRIFE

Civil conflicts in Ireland, Russia, the Indian subcontinent, the Balkans, Cambodia and Africa – the causes and effects of civil war around the world

Cyprus, 1964

Following years of resistance to British rule, Cyprus gained its independence from Britain in 1960. Violence as a result of tensions between the Greek Cypriot majority and the Turkish Cypriot minority broke out in 1963 in the capital Nicosia. Although UN peacekeepers were deployed in 1964, continuing violence forced most Turkish Cypriots into enclaves throughout the island. Subsequently an attempted Greek coup in 1974 provoked a Turkish invasion which led to the creation of the Turkish Republic of Northern Cyprus, recognized only by Turkey. The latest attempt at a UN settlement plan was rejected by Greek Cypriots in a referendum in April 2004. As a result in May 2004 only the Greek Cypriot Republic of Cyprus became a member of the European Community. Although all Cypriots are now European citizens, EU laws do not apply in northern, Turkish Cyprus.

British troops, Northern Ireland, October 1969

1967 saw the setting up of the Northern Ireland Civil Rights Association (NICRA) which organized civil rights protests, but the organization was branded a front for the Irish Republican Army (IRA) by the government in Stormont and its marches were banned. The heavy-handed dispersal of a NICRA march in Londonderry by the Royal Ulster Constabulary (RUC) in October 1968 and an attack on a People's Democracy march in January 1969 led to heightened tensions between Catholics and Protestants. By August 1969, after the marching season – beginning with the Drumcree Parade of the Orange Order at Portadown – these had deepened and Catholics rioted and fought with the RUC for three days in western Derry in what became known as the Battle of the Bogside. In Belfast entire streets were burned down and over 3,500 families, mostly Catholic, were driven from their homes. Seven people died and one hundred were injured.

Northern Ireland, October 1969

Northern Ireland's Catholic minority welcomed British troops when they were first sent to the province in August 1969 in response to an upsurge in sectarian violence. Around the same time the Provisional IRA broke away from the main body of the IRA which it criticized for its failure to protect Catholic enclaves. Northern Ireland would still have its troubles when the young boy seen in the photograph with his toy gun had grown to adulthood.

Age of innocence, Northern Ireland

An earlier, innocent time in relationships between British troops in Northern Ireland and its Catholic minority. Although, given subsequent events, it seems scarcely credible, British troops were cheered by the Catholic community of Londonderry they had come to protect in late 1969. This young girl would not have been scolded or shamed by her family for speaking to the 'enemy' and the soldier taking a tea break would have had no cause to view the child as a potential threat. Subsequent events were increasingly to make this kind of scene a distant memory.

British troops on the Falls Road, Belfast

Seen here in flames in 1969, the Falls Road was to become known around the world in the years that followed. Along with the Protestant Shankill Road, also in west Belfast, the Catholic Falls Road was to be one of the key sites of Northern Ireland's 'troubles'. This photograph dates from the early days of the British government's decision to deploy troops on the streets of Ireland. In response to the emergence of the Provisional IRA as a force in Northern Ireland politics, the British became convinced of the need to introduce internment. It was at a a NICRA rally against internment on Sunday 30 January 1972 that the British Army shot dead thirteen demonstrators and injured another fourteen. That day which was to become known as 'Bloody Sunday' marked the end of the use of mass demonstrations in an attempt to win civil rights.

Unidentified dead, India-Pakistan War, 1971

Unidentified dead lie on the railway tracks as the Indian Army, having taken the key city of Jessore in Bangladesh, approaches the capital Dhaka. During the partition of India, Muslim Pakistan gained independence in 1947, created out of Muslim majority territories in the west and the east. Initially, Pakistan was divided into West Pakistan and East Bengal or East Pakistan. Actions by Pakistan's army against rebels in East Pakistan led to the exodus of up to eight million Hindus into India as their land was given to Bangladeshi peasants in an attempt to placate them. Indian prime minister Indira Gandhi decided that India's only option was to support the rebels in their fight against Pakistan leading to the war of 1971 and the creation of Bangladesh.

Bangladesh, 20 December 1971

Prisoners are searched following India's victory in the India-Pakistan War of 1971. It was feared that there would be reprisals, but these did not materialise to any great extent. Although between 300,000 and a million people are thought to have died during the war, the new state was fairly swiftly accepted by the world despite initial objections from Pakistan's ally, China.

Revenge in Kulna, India–Pakistan War, 1971

Following India's swift victory in the India–Pakistan War of 1971, residents revenge themselves in the town of Kulna in what had been East Pakistan, or East Bengal, but was to become the new state of Bangladesh.

Khmer Rouge killing fields

Bones lie in a shallow grave near Angkor Wat in Cambodia, the remains of victims of the Khmer Rouge, the Cambodian communist organization led by Pol Pot that is thought to have been responsible for the deaths of up to 1.5 million Cambodians. The Khmer Rouge insurgency began in 1970 and rapidly gained control over two thirds of the country. From 3,000 members in 1970, the strength of the Khmer Rouge had increased to 30,000 by 1973. In 1975, it overthrew the government and established Democratic Kampuchea. In the years to come cities were evacuated, schools and factories closed and the Cambodian people were compelled to work on collective farms. Intellectuals and skilled workers were the first to be killed, but many more were to die from causes including starvation and forced marches before the final dissolution of Khmer Rouge in 1999. Pol Pot died in April 1998 and Khieu Samphan, who had already succeeded him, surrendered in December of the same year.

The home of Hasreta Ahmic, Bosnia

Burnt corpses lie in the home of Hasreta Ahmic in the village of Ahmici in Bosnia. On 16 April 1993, Croat forces shelled Ahmici, then moved from house to house killing women, children, infants and livestock, destroying houses and barns. Every Muslim home in the village was burned. It is believed that 110 people were killed in the attack.

Rebuilding Bosnia's bridges, Sipovo

Royal Engineers work to repair a footbridge near Sipovo, to the north-west of Sarajevo in Bosnia. Destroyed during the war, the bridge had connected five villages and served as the main crossing point for over 400 Bosnian-Serb and Bosniac men, women and children. Without the bridge people were compelled to make a twelve-kilometre round trip to Sipovo for basic necessities and children faced a very long walk to school.

A sniper of the Kosovo Liberation Army, Kosovo, May 1999

In 1990, ethnic Albanians declared the independence of Kosovo from Serbia leading to the election of Ibrahim Rugova as president of the self-proclaimed republic in 1992. Ethnic tension and armed unrest escalated until open conflict between the Serb police and the separatist Kosovo Liberation Army in 1998 led to a brutal crackdown by Serb forces. In response to the Serb rejection of an internationally brokered agreement signed by the Kosovo Albanians, Nato launched air strikes against Yugoslavia. In 1999, President Milosevic withdrew Serb troops from Kosovo, Nato's air strikes were called off and the UN's Kosovo Peace Implementation Force (KFOR) and Nato forces arrived in Kosovo leading to the KLA agreeing to disarm.

Komogllave, Kosovo, 1999

Taibe Ilazie cries in her home in Komgllave, Kosovo, destroyed by Serb forces.

British paratroopers guard renegade KLA fighters, Kosovo, Pristina

British paratroopers guard ethnic Albanian KLA fighters who had been attempting to terrorise Serb families in flats in Pristina, Kosovo. To many, the greatest achievement of Josip Tito who led Yugoslavia, of which Kosovo was a part, from 1945 to 1980, was to suppress nationalist insurrections and maintain unity. His death brought speculation as to whether Yugoslavia could be kept intact by his successors. In the post-Tito era, ethnic divisions and conflict grew and finally erupted in a series of wars a decade after Tito's death which pitted neighbours who had lived side by side for decades against one another and resulted in the dissolution of Yugoslavia.

Repairing a home, Kosovo, 1999

Ilmi Pareva working to repair the chimney of his home in Pristina, Kosovo in December 1999. Pristina was extensively damaged during the war, in part by Nato air strikes.

Refugees return to Rwanda, 1996

Rwanda's existence has been bedevilled by the unequal relationship between a dominant Tutsi minority and a Hutu majority. This situation was reversed after 1959 when a civil war caused about 200,000 Tutsis to flee to Burundi. Subsequent periodic massacres of Tutsis took place, but the most notorious, which led to the slaughter of an estimated 800,000 Tutsis and moderate Hutus took place in April 1994 following the death of President Juvenal Habyarimana and the president of Burundi when the plane carrying them was shot down. In response the Tutsi-led Rwandan Patriotic Front launched a military campaign to take control of the country. Around two million Hutus fled to the Democratic Republic of the Congo (then Zaire) with many others fleeing to other neighbouring countries. Though reluctantly, fearing reprisals, many refugees began to return in 1996.

Burundi Army in action against
Hutu rebels, 2000

Burundian soldiers on patrol along the Rwandan border mime a grenade attack on a bus which had taken place the previous night. In December 2005, a major offensive by Burundi's army killed 120 fighters from the only remaining Hutu rebel group and captured 646. Burundi has been engaged in a long-running civil war between rebels from its Hutu majority in the form of the Forces for National Liberation (FNL) and the Tutsi elite that has killed 300,000 people since 1993.

A Rwandan Interahamwe guerilla captured by the Burundian army, 2000

A Rwandan Interahamwe guerilla, shot in the jaw and severely beaten about the face – captured by the Burundian patrol pictured earlier – sits up in a military hospital and reaches for a pen and paper to write a confession. In the Kinyarwanda language spoken in Rwanda Interahamwe means 'those who stand (or fight) together'; the Interahamwe were the largest Hutu militia, responsible for much of the killing in Rwanda in 1994. Following the Rwandan Patriotic Front victory, many Interahamwe members fled to Zaire and other countries bordering Rwanda, including Burundi. In August 2004, Interahamwe fighters killed 150 Tutsi refugees in a United Nations refugee camp in Burundi. Following the recruitment of a number of Congolese Hutu, the Interahamwe now calls itself the Armèe de Libèration du Rwanda.

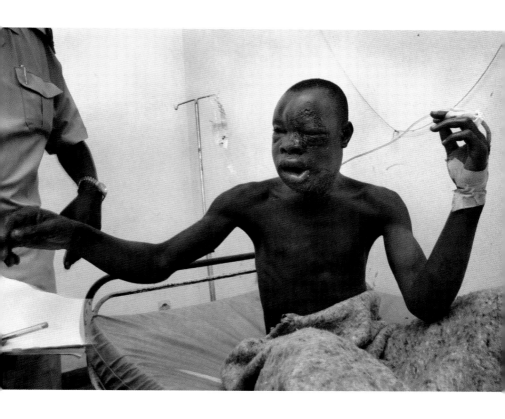

Krinding refugee camp, West Darfur, Sudan

In March 2003 fighting broke out in the Darfur region of western Sudan between government forces and rebels from the Sudan Liberation Army (SLA) and the Justice and Equality Movement (JEM). The resulting conflict in Darfur is ongoing between the government-backed, Arab Janjaweed militia, and the non-Arab people of the region, though some – including the Sudanese government – understand the struggle as between settled farmers and nomadic herders in competition for scarce resources and dispute any attempt to label the struggle as ethnic cleansing or genocide. An estimated 1.8 million people have been forced to flee their homes and villages and estimates of the number of people killed range from 50,000 to 300,000 since the conflict began, mostly through starvation. Krinding refugee camp is home to 23,000 Internally Displaced People (IDPs).

PART THREE

A WORLD AT WAR

*The Second World War – rearmament in the
1930s – the outbreak of hostilities – the Home
Front – conflict in Europe and North Africa – the
war in the Pacific – the final battles*

Hawker Hurricanes rehearsing for
Empire Flying Day, 1938

As the drift towards war in Europe became irreversible, the arms race
assumed a great importance. Domestic and financial constraints had meant
that Britain and France lagged behind the German war machine, but in the
late 1930s they started to narrow the gap.

The construction of aeroplanes such as Hawker Hurricanes, pictured here
rehearsing for Empire Flying Day over Kent in 1938, accelerated. Two years
later the same aircraft would be defending London and the South East
against German bombing during the Battle of Britain. This faster pace of
European rearmament led Hitler to launch attacks on France in 1940 and
Russia in 1941 earlier than he might otherwise have preferred to.

Soldier kissing child goodbye, October 1939

In October 1939, a British soldier kisses his young child goodbye. The period from September 1939 when war was declared to April 1940 is often referred to as the 'phoney war' although Churchill called it the 'twilight war' and the Germans the 'Sitzkrieg' (the sitting war). While preparation continued and many joined the armed forces in training, there was relatively little news of major impact on the public. There were naval skirmishes, and the occupation of Poland meant the citizens of that country could not regard this as phoney warfare, but on the wider stage this was a period of relative calm before the storm.

Fairey Battle bombers

Not all of the British aircraft production was of the necessary standard. The Fairey Battle, produced at Heaton Chapel, was a single-engined bomber. The Fairey Battles were a large part of the Advance Air Striking Force used in the early stages of the war. Britain's first success in the air war came when a Battle (K9293) shot down a German Messerschmitt Bf109 in the skies of France. However the Battle was too slow, with a maximum speed of 250 mph, too big for its single 768kW Rolls-Royce Merlin I engine and not sufficiently well armed. The planes were mostly diverted to training purposes for the duration of the war. In 2001 a Royal Air Force team undertook a mission to retrieve the bodies of four airmen whose Fairey Battle crashed into an Icelandic glacier in May 1941 after getting lost in fog. The men were left in the ice because of the difficulty at the time of recovering the bodies from the mountainside, and it was sixty years before the location of the craft was discovered by a local historian.

The German occupation of Paris, 1940

The French had relied heavily on the Maginot Line to defend them from any possible attack by the Germans. While the fortifications of the Line in general were hard to breach there were errors in the planning of the defence. Firstly the Ardennes Forest was left as a gap in the line on the assumption that it was impassable for a serious military force. Secondly the treaty with Belgium that France had held until the late thirties meant that the Line was not built there until the late thirties, and then not to the high specifications of the rest of the line. The German invasion of 1940 came through the Low Countries and also through the Ardennes Forest and was overwhelming and decisive.

On 13 June, Paris was evacuated by French forces, in the face of the advancing German army. In this picture, German forces pass through the Arc de Triomphe on the Champs Elysees. France surrendered on 23 June. The surrender committed them to the disarmament of French forces and the occupation of two-thirds of France by the Germans, while the Vichy government ruled a rump state in the south.

Dunkirk, 1940

The British Expeditionary Force (BEF) returning from Dunkirk. The German drive into France separated the bulk of the French and British forces, leaving the British stranded on the north-west coast. By late May 1940 the British forces were cornered, and after a long retreat the bulk of the British Expeditionary Force reached the Dunkirk bridgehead. On 26 May, 'Operation Dynamo' – the evacuation – began.

The Royal Air Force, bitterly maligned at the time by the Army (the respect they later attained came about as a result of the Battle of Britain), fought vehemently to deny the enemy the total air supremacy that would have destroyed the BEF. It was hoped that some 45,000 men could be evacuated. In the event 338,000 allied troops were saved, 26,000 of whom were French. On 4 June, Churchill reported to the House of Commons, seeking to check the mood of national euphoria and relief at the unexpected deliverance. This was after all a defeat, even though it could have been much worse. His speech became known as 'We shall fight them on the beaches.'

Funeral for victims of an air raid, Portsmouth

As the British were driven out of Europe by the Nazi expansion, the situation was fairly grim. German bombing raids, intended as the prelude to an eventual invasion, harried towns and cities across the country. Here, a mass funeral is held for victims of an air raid in Portsmouth.

View through a bomb aimer's sights on a raid over Germany

Bombing of civilian targets was not widely regarded as a legitimate strategy at the start of the war. The first British bombing raids on Germany were to drop leaflets in an attempt to influence German public opinion, and also to demonstrate the ease with which bombers could get through.

It seems to have been an accident that caused the greatest change in this tactic. A lost German bomber ditched its bombs on an area of London. Churchill ordered Bomber Command (the specialist bombing unit set up in 1936) to retaliate with a minor raid on Berlin. But this enraged Hitler to the point that he ordered the destruction of British cities, thus leading on to the Blitz (and indirectly to later horrors such as the bombing of Dresden).

At first Bomber Command concentrated on daylight raids, aiming for precision targeting of strategic targets. But too many aircraft were lost to air defences in daylight so the strategy switched to night raids. This created great difficulty in targeting (it was not uncommon for raids to entirely miss the city they were aiming for). This photograph, taken through an RAF bomb aimer's window gives a hint of the difficulty and danger involved in such raids, as well as showing the indiscriminate destruction wrought at ground level.

German paratroopers

The increased importance of air forces in the Second World War created some different options for strategists. While the first world war had ground to a halt in the mud, the use of advance forces of paratroopers seemed to offer ways of jumping ahead and creating pincer movements on opposing forces, and perhaps of transporting invasion forces across water. However there were limitations to the new technology. Most paratroopers at the time used round parachutes. These had limited steering, via the straps that attached the harness to the connectors and suspension lines. The Germans adopted the use of paratroops at an early stage, but German paratroopers used more primitive versions of round parachutes, with only a single riser at the back of the harness, meaning that there was no steering capability. Also, the largest German cargo aircraft available, the Ju-52, could not take many more than twenty paratroopers at a time. As a result the use of German paratroops as an advance assault force was only effective in limited engagements, although there was some fear in Britain of a mass parachute drop that might trigger a German invasion.

Kite balloons above shipping, 1942

Kite balloons flying above British ships in April 1942. Kite balloons were much used in the First World War, both as observation posts and as decoys or obstacles to low-flying aircraft. The RAF had a Kite Balloon Section specifically dedicated to their creation and servicing. The shape of the balloon created stability and aerodynamic lift from the wind. Wires and even explosives hung from the balloons created additional obstacles for aircraft. A considerable number of aircraft were destroyed by Kite Balloons during the war, thought they were most effective as a deterrent against attack.

A child being rescued during the Clydebank Blitz

The Blitz in London, and the bombing in towns such as Coventry may be more widely documented, but Clydebank in Scotland suffered some of the worst devastation in Britain in relation to its size. The town, on the outskirts of Glasgow, was an important industrial and shipbuilding base. On 13 March 1941, Clydebank came under attack from over 200 German bombers, the first air raid the town had experienced. The first attack lasted all night and involved a variety of bombs including incendiaries and high explosive bombs. The incendiary bombs caused the worst damage. The following night an identical attack was launched, resulting in more destruction and casualties.

Clydebank was in a state of near destruction following the bombing and one could still see traces of the bomb sites many years later – some might say the town never fully recovered. In two nights, 528 died, over 600 were seriously injured, and many more suffered from minor injuries. The town was evacuated, with over 48,000 refugees leaving the town.

Women in gasmasks

Chemical gas had been used sporadically during the First World War and was greatly feared, even though it had rarely been an effective battlefield weapon. Gasmasks were issued early on to the British population, and an attempt was made to encourage the population to carry them with them at all times to be prepared for possible civilian gas attacks – by 1940, 38 million masks had been issued, including special ones for children and even babies. Of course it might not have been wise to continue with a cooking exhibition in the event of an actual attack, but the message conveyed was that it was perfectly normal to wear masks in everyday situations. Fortunately, while civilian bombing became commonplace during this conflict, gas was not in fact used by either side.

Hitler had in fact developed nerve gases, including Sarin. Other participants in the conflict, including Russia and the USA also developed advanced chemical agents during the period. There are conflicting reports about Hitler's reluctance to use his supplies of nerve gas. He had experienced the use of gas in the First World War and knew of its potentially debilitating effects. But in the end the argument was probably won by those that argued that any German use of gas would be met by similar weapons from the other side, and that this was a risk not worth taking.

A British raid on a German base in Norway, 1941

On 27 December 1941, British Commandos launched a raid on German bases in Norway landing on the coast at Vaagso and Maaloy Islands. The Commandos were formed in June 1940 as an irregular and unconventional raider force, intended to attack and disrupt enemy forces in unpredictable ways. Many of the attacks they carried out were aimed at diverting enemy resources from other areas, or at disrupting supply lines. Their operations also served to demoralize and confuse enemy forces. The Commandos quickly attained a celebrity status comparable to that enjoyed by fighter pilots with the public.

This raid was supported by air cover from the RAF and a Royal Navy force. Following a barrage from the air and sea, the commandos landed with a specific list of target operations to fulfil. It was a largely successful raid, although they encountered much heavier street fighting than expected in South Vaagso, as the troop presence there was stronger than anticipated. Nonetheless four factories, a fish oil store, the telephone exchange and several military installations were destroyed or damaged.

The raid convinced Hitler that the British were planning a wider invasion in Scandinavia, leading him to commit 30,000 troops and a significant naval detachment to the area, thereby diverting these forces from other strategically more significant areas.

Survivors of the Bismarck, 1941

Survivors of the sinking of the Bismarck pictured alongside HMS Dorsetshire. On 27 May 1941, the Bismarck was sunk after a relentless three-day hunt by ships of the Royal Navy. The Bismarck was the pride of Germany's fleet, one of the strongest battleships of its day, over 35,000 tons, and this was her first voyage.

There was by this stage a de facto co-operation between US and British naval forces and US surveillance assisted the British during Atlantic operations. The Bismarck had managed to sink the HMS Hood with great loss of life in the first engagement between the two sides. Over 1,400 British sailors died and only three survived. However Bismarck had taken a hole in its bow, which slowed it down, and the long pursuit ensued. Aircraft from the Ark Royal slowed the Bismarck as the British fleet closed in.

Once the rudder of the Bismarck was damaged by a torpedo, it was effectively crippled, and repeated assaults and bombardments gradually destroyed the ship. Eventually the great ship sank (or was scuttled by the remaining crew according to some recent accounts) some 500 miles west of Land's End. This was a blow to German morale, but was treated as a great victory in Britain, at a time when the war was being lost. Most of the Bismarck's crew of over 2,000 were lost but 115 managed to survive, including these lucky few.

Captured U-boat, 1941

Only three of the German's feared U-boats were captured during the Second World War – U-110, U-505 and U-570, the first U-boat to be captured intact, pictured here. U-570 was captured on 27 August 1941 following a depth charge attack by aircraft off Iceland. The U-570 was taken to Barrow for a refit by local shipbuilders. One local welder was brave enough to cut the live torpedos from the damaged hull of the boat, which had to be done before any further work could be undertaken. The boat was examined for its technical secrets, many of which were in advance of British capabilities at that stage. She was renamed HMS Graph and went on to years of active service, including the sinking of another U-boat, U-333.

The sinking of HMS Ark Royal, 1941

The crew of the stricken ship is rescued as HMS Ark Royal begins to list prior to sinking, on 13 November 1941. HMS Ark Royal was an important ship in the British fleet, with a revolutionary design for aircraft carrying that became the prototype for all future British aircraft carriers. She was often in the headlines and received many battle honours. One of the ship's Blackburn Skuas was responsible for the first enemy aircraft to be shot down by a Fleet Air Arm aircraft in September 1939, and then on 10 April 1940 her aircraft sank the German cruiser Konigsberg – the first major vessel to be sunk by air attack in this way. The end came when she was hit by a torpedo from German submarine U-81 off Gibraltar.

The sinking was slow, and HMS Ark Royal was being towed towards port when, thirteen hours after being hit, and just twenty miles from Gibraltar, the ship capsized and sank.

Canadian troops leaving ship for shore

The Canadian involvement in the Second World War was strong from the start. In the First World War Britain's declaration of war obliged Canada to join in. By 1939 this was no longer the case, but there was strong support for the fight against the Germans, and many Canadians joined up in the early part of the war. By 1941, there were 250,000 Canadian troops fighting, including two fighter squadrons and the Canadian Navy, which participated in the Atlantic War.

The Dieppe raid, 1942

Soldiers killed during the Dieppe raid lie on the beach surrounded by a damaged tank and a burning landing craft. The worst single day of loss for Canada in the second world war was this disastrous raid in August 1942, when Canadian troops and British Commandos attacked the northern French town. The operation was allegedly undertaken partly because of a request from the Soviet Union who were suffering from a ferocious Nazi assault, and hoped that the allies might be able to provide a distraction on the Western front. Of 5,000 Canadian troops involved, over 800 died and a further 2,000 were captured.

Some have characterized the raid as no more that a botched military operation, but others have argued that the lessons learnt from this raid were crucial in the planning of the eventually successful Normandy landings.

Another consequence of the raid came about because of the seizure of the battle plan from one officer, who incorrectly took this into the operation with him. The Germans interpreted part of the battle plan as an instruction for Commandos to shackle prisoners, and issued instructions for Canadians in captivity to be so shackled (provoking a retaliatory response from the British and Canadians, although neither order was fully carried out). More seriously this controversy led indirectly to Hitler signing the Commando Order, an instruction that rather than imprisoning special forces operators such as the Commandos, they were henceforth to be executed. The Germans had been discomfited by the actions of Commandos and had concentrated propaganda efforts on discrediting their methods – the Dieppe battle plan merely provided an excuse for them to take more extreme action.

Soldiers of the 8th Army wash in the sea

Machine gun protection for soldiers from the British 8th Army as they wash in the sea. The North African conflict was very different to the war in Europe. It served to deflect Axis resources from other fronts and also defended crucial supply lines and strategic points from falling. But in the end it also provided some of the most crucial turning points of the war in events such as the siege of Tobruk and the battle of El Alamein.

El Alamein, 1943

The victory at El Alamein, in 1943, under the leadership of Montgomery was one of several crucial turning points of the entire war, as it allowed the allies to turn back Axis forces in the area and to start to establish bridgeheads from which to push back up into Europe from the south. Montgomery took command of the 8th Army in August 1942, and prepared a detailed plan to beat the German forces with overpowering force. Prior to this the North African campaign had been a series of advances and retreats with few conclusive engagements. El Alamein changed that. On 23 October, the British started a massive artillery barrage which pinned the heavily fortified German units in place. By 2 November, Rommel was asking to retreat, hoping to save his army as he had on previous occasions. However he was ordered by Hitler to stand his ground regardless of the risks. German units fled, leaving more than 30,000 infantry to surrender. This gave the British their first large-scale land victory of the war.

A light machine-gun crew from the Belgian Congo

A light machine-gun crew from the Belgian Congo undergoing intensive training at Port Tewfik, on the Suez Canal, their first camp in the Middle East. As in the First World War, the Allied forces were dependent on Africa for both manpower and resources. Especially with the Asian markets cut off from trade, Africa assumed a great significance. In addition, Hitler was determined eventually to recapture the colonies that had been confiscated from the Germans following the First World War.

Half a million Africans fought on the French and English side in the war. There were extensive propaganda efforts on both sides devoted to winning over the local populations. Many Africans had seen Mussolini's invasion of Ethiopia as an unwarranted act of aggression and this fueled Allied recruitment. The Belgian government, in exile in London, placed Belgian units into the British Armed Forces and put the Belgian Congo's vast resources, including many vital minerals, at the disposal of the Allied war effort.

Beaufighter bombers

At the outset of the war, Britain was lacking in long-range heavy fighters. Aircraft such as the Spitfire and the Hurricane were ideally designed for short-range missions, but it became clear that a longer-range craft was needed.

The Beaufighter was designed and constructed in a remarkably short time frame by the Bristol Company. The Ministry of Defence put in an order for 300 of the plane, as yet unbuilt, in late 1938. By July 1939 a prototype was up and running, a twin-engined bomber, and by autumn of 1940 the final version was available for long-range missions. This was a crucial weapon in the stage of the war during which the allies' land bases were far-flung and remote from their required targets. The plane was used as a night fighter and as a long-range strike aircraft, and also saw heavy service in North Africa, Burma and the Far East.

American soldier washing in the snow

An American soldier stripped to the waist in the snow washes himself near his 105 Howitzer on the Western front, France, in the winter of 1944–45. The USA entered the conflict following the Japanese attack on Pearl Harbor. Initially declaring war on Japan in response to the attack, the US involvement in the European conflict became inevitable once Germany and Italy declared war on the US. The destruction of the Pearl Harbor fleet gave Japan an initial advantage in the Pacific War. As the US geared up for the global conflict in terms of recruitment and industrial support, they initially struggled in the Pacific and Japan overran large areas of south-east Asia. However the US turned the tide in the Battle of Midway in June 1942, with a decisive attack on the Japanese fleet, an attack that relied on bombers taking off from aircraft carriers for the final blow.

In Europe, the US deployed huge numbers of troops and equipment to the UK. As the tide slowly started to turn in the conflict, US troops were crucial parts of the Allied invasions of North Africa in 1942, Sicily and Italy in 1943, and France in 1944. This picture is taken in the later stages of the war as the allied armies in Northern Europe started to push the Nazi forces back into Germany.

B-26 Marauders of the US 9th Air Force

B-26 Marauders of the US 9th Air Force seen here heading home after a raid on occupied Europe were engaged in heavy strategic bombing of Nazi Germany. The B-26 was developed in 1940 as part of the US armaments program. With a range of just 1,000 miles, its earliest missions were from US bases in Australia into the Pacific theatre. Initially there were safety issues with the bomber, and several adjustments had to be made to the design of the craft. The US had hoped to be able to fly unaccompanied bombing missions with the B-26, but the losses on these missions were too high, and the B-26 was at its most effective in 1944 when, with suitable accompanying fighter planes, the B-26s in Europe supported the advancing allied armies following the D-Day landings.

A sailor kisses his girl goodbye

A sailor kisses a girl goodbye as he leaves for active service. The intense circumstances of global warfare led to many emotional and moral changes in society. Husbands and wives, and lovers knew that any departure might be their last, and this, together with the increased role played by women in public life in a society where many men were away fighting, led to ongoing change in social mores. The immense popularity of songs such as 'Every Time We Say Goodbye', and 'We'll Meet Again' was largely because of the way they captured this charged mood of fearful romance.

A B-25 Mitchell bomber of the USAAF attacking Cassino, 1944

As Allied forces fought their way up Italy, the battles of Monte Cassino were some of the key points at which the advance was halted. The Axis troops held the Gustav line, and Monte Cassino was a crucial strategic point, one that has been involved in many battles going back into antiquity for this reason. The castle and monastery were heavily fortified, and repeated allied attempts to take the town failed – in the first three battles of Monte Cassino from January to March 1944, 54,000 men from the USA, UK, India, New Zealand, Australia and Canada lost their lives.

The fourth battle, in May 1944, led by a Polish regiment, with support from Indian gunners, Moroccan forces and British troops took two massive assaults to capture the monastery and town. The monastery and town were both completely destroyed in the fighting – the town has been rebuilt, but the historic buildings of the monastery could not be. The dreadful fighting of these battles had finally opened the gate to Rome, which fell on 4 June, just days before the Normandy landings opened up the battle in France.

German and Italian soldiers surrendering

German and Italian soldiers carrying a white flag and with their arms raised surrender to an Allied soldier.

A Japanese ammunition dump is blown up in the central Pacific, 1944

A mushroom cloud rises from the Japanese ammunition dump on Kwajalein Atoll in the Marshall Islands in the central Pacific after being hit by bombs from US planes in early 1944. Kwajalein was occupied by American forces later in 1944 and repaired. It was used a base for B-24 bombers of the 7th Air Force, flying missions to Wake, Truk and beyond. The nature of warfare in the Pacific at this stage of the war led to the US strategy of island-hopping, whereby heavily fortified enemy positions were skipped in the progress towards Japan, and limited resources were instead focused on strategically useful islands that had fewer defences, but could serve as bases.

This strategy worked because the US was operating an effective submarine blockade, which made it hard for the Japanese to adapt by shifting troops from one island to another. One consequence was the phenomena of hold-outs, in which stranded Japanese troops refused to believe that the war was over, and continued to maintain their positions until long after the official surrender in 1945.

US bombers attack Seleo Island, New Guinea

In the Pacific war, Australian forces often fought alongside US forces. Here, Australian soldiers watch as US bombers provide support by bombing Seleo Island in New Guinea. A naval attack on Port Moresby in New Guinea in May 1942 was repelled by Allied navies, on of the first setbacks the Japanese suffered. The capture of Port Moresby would have been strategically important for Japan, as it would have provided them with a base within reach of Australia itself. Following the Battle of Midway, a land attack on Port Moresby was launched. In an extraordinary rearguard action, the inexperienced Australian 39th battalion defeated 5,000 Japanese troops.

On 7 August that year, while US forces fought an extensive battle at Guadalcanal, a further Japanese attack on the eastern tip of New Guinea was driven back by the now reinforced Australian forces at Milne Bay. This, together with the subsequent Japanese defeat at Guadalcanal marked the turning point in this region as Japanese forces suffered their first reverses. The Japanese had planned to use Guadalcanal, in the Solomon Islands as a base from which to cut off naval links between the USA and Australasia – the fact that American forces, with assistance from the forces of Australia and New Zealand were able to prevent this was crucial in the strategic development of the Pacific war.

Canadian troops landing in France, 1944

On 6 June the invasion of France was finally launched. The first waves of troops landing faced terrible odds, and many died from enemy fire in the course of the landing. Canadian forces landing at Juno Beach suffered 50% casualties, the second highest of the D-Day beaches. However, in spite of setbacks here and elsewhere, by the end of the first day, 155,000 troops from Canada, Britain and America had succeeded in taking a small band of territory along the coast, a band that would be broadened over subsequent days.

Behind the first lines of combat troops, a major support operation delivered subsequent waves of troops to the same beaches over the following days, as the battle for France began.

Allied troops on the Normandy invasion beaches, 1944

Allied troops stand among the ammunition boxes and supplies on the Normandy invasion beaches. Beaches which only days earlier had been the scene of fierce fighting now became the scene of a major logistical effort, devoted to ensuring that the troops fighting their way east were supported and supplied with food, water, supplies, and ammunition.

US cemetery, Omaha

The landings at Omaha Beach are remembered as some of the bloodiest of D-day – over 2,000 American troops died in the initial wave of landings. Omaha was a critical beach where 100-foot high cliffs overlooked three and a half miles of sand, stretching from Sainte Honorine-des-Pertes to Veireville-sur-Mer. Unfortunately for the attackers, the German 716th Coastal Defence Division had been reinforced by the 352nd Infantry Division, who were there for an exercise on that day, thus doubling the troops available for defence of the beach.

The 1st and 29th American infantry divisions, reinforced by companies of rangers, made up the attacking force. There were a number of problems with the planning of the attack. Amphibious tanks that were to supply crucial defensive fire were launched too far from the shore and many sank or became flooded. The allied air bombardment largely overshot targets, while the naval bombardment made insufficient impact on the German lines, and the defences on the beach were still close to full strength when the first wave landed. As a result many were killed instantly or as they attempted to shift wet equipment up on to the beach.

General Omar Bradley considered abandoning the attack, but gradually a few minor breakthroughs were made by those lucky enough to survive. Some of the landing craft had managed to hit shore in between defensive positions where fire was less concentrated, and a few units managed to take ground from which they could attack the German defences. Meanwhile the naval bombardment became more effective as allied destroyers risked running aground to get close enough to provide effective cover for the exposed troops. Robert Capa, the great photographer, was on Omaha in the second wave of landings, returning shortly afterwards in a landing craft – unfortunately, most of his pictures were apparently lost in a darkroom accident.

In the end Omaha was secured, but at a terrible cost of life. The cemetery covers 172 acres, and was donated by France. It is a moving memorial to the bravery of those who gave their lives.

Planes of the US 12th Air Force dropping supplies for Nice/Marseilles beachhead

The importance of the beachhead in southern France has often been underestimated by historians of the Second World War, and was disputed even at the time. Churchill fiercely opposed the landings during the planning in early 1944, feeling that they only served to take resources from the Italian campaign, and the planned Normandy landings. Operation Anvil, as it was called, was at one point cancelled, but as it became clear that the Normandy forces were in a temporary stalemate as they attempted to fight their way clear of the coast, it became more obvious that the supply chain would be an ongoing problem. The allied forces had very few northern ports they could rely on, until the capture of Antwerp later that year.

Anvil was launched on 15 August 1944, with the first landings taking place near St Tropez. The forces involved were predominantly American, Canadian and Free French, and the main objective was to capture towns such as Toulon and Marseilles, and to move north to capture the Rhone Valley. The landings were successful at quickly establishing a beachhead and, with Commando forces causing disruption to German bases, it soon became apparent that the Allied forces were in a strong position. Within days the German forces were withdrawing from the area, pursued rapidly by Allied units, leaving forces to defend only strategically significant towns in the south. By 28 August, Marseilles and Toulon had fallen, and the roads to the north were starting to be secured. This provided vital supply lines to Eisenhower's forces in the north, and also ensured that the armies fighting their way from Normandy east were not harried on their southern flanks by German forces.

British troops celebrate victory in France, 1944

After the Normandy landings, the Allied troops found themselves in tremendously difficult terrain, faced with fierce resistance. After over a month of slow progress, the Allied troops started to make progress when Operation Cobra succeeded and allowed the start of the St Lo breakout on 24 July 1944. From there, progress accelerated, and a swathe of northern France soon fell, culminating in the liberation of Paris on 25 August.

V2 bomb damage in Leytonstone, London, 1944

Local resident Mrs Berbiest gathers her belongings from the remains of her home at Mornington Road Junction in Leytonstone, London after a V2 rocket attack in November 1944. Four people died in this attack, which may have been aimed at anti-aircraft guns on Wanstead Flats, or at the nearby railway. Over 500 V2s landed in London between September 1944 and March 1945 spreading fear in a population who had already suffered from years of conventional bombing.

The V1s (doodlebugs) had already been used with terrifying effect in Britain. Also named from the German word for revenge, Vergeltungswaffe, the V2s were the first true rockets, developed by Werner von Braun. V1s had given a late screaming noise which gave a few seconds warning, but the speed of V2s meant that they were deadly weapons that killed without warning. They were regarded as unreliable by Nazi chiefs, and might have been developed sooner with more support in the hierarchy. Eisenhower believed that if the V2 had been available sooner, the Normandy invasion would have been more difficult, if not impossible. A V2 blitz on Antwerp in late 1944 did much to damage supply lines to Eisenhower's forces.

The effectiveness of V2 attacks was gradually diminished through 1945 as advancing allied forces captured the launch sites.

The Camel Corps of the King's African Rifles in Somaliland, 1945

In the aftermath of the war in North Africa, the Camel Corps of the King's African Rifles are pictured here in October 1945, flying the Union Jack on the Abyssinian frontier of British Somaliland. A border patrol of the Camel Corps led by a British officer is operating within the confines of the protectorate. The tree stands in Abyssinian territory.

St Paul's Cathedral, floodlit to celebrate VE Day, 1945

St Paul's Cathedral, floodlit during the VE Day celebrations to celebrate the Allied victory in Europe in May 1945. After years of struggle, the people of Europe were finally able to look forward with some degree of hope to a new world. The war in the Pacific ended three months later in August 1945 when Japan surrendered following the atomic bombs that were dropped on Hiroshima and Nagasaki.

PART FOUR

THE AGE OF SUPERPOWERS

The Atomic Age – the Cold War and conflict in Korea – rebellion in the Eastern Bloc – the Cuban Missile Crisis – the Vietnam War

Gurkhas witnessing atomic test

British Gurkha soldiers observing a mushroom cloud as part of a 1962 nuclear exercise. The British first tested a nuclear weapon in 1957, and exercises with actual weapons took place on or near Pacific Islands and in Australia – Australian soldiers sought compensation from the British government in 2001 for allegedly using them as guinea pigs in the 1950s by exposing them to dangerous radiation as part of the testing program. From 1962 onwards, British tests were conducted at the underground range in Nevada.

US marines under attack in the Korean War, 1950

The Korean War started in 1950 when, following a series of border incidents, the Stalinist regime of North Korea invaded the South, whose security had only recently been maintained by US forces following the Second World War. By October, the US (and UN) forces had driven the North Koreans back deep into their own territory and were nearing the Manchurian border. General MacArthur met with President Truman on Wake Island to assure him that victory was in sight, and that war would be all but over by Christmas.

However the proximity of UN forces to the Chinese border provoked the newly communist country into reacting, and Chinese forces poured into Korea from November. The UN forces were pushed back through December and by the New Year had been forced to the South of Seoul. This image captures marines of the 5th and 7th US regiments, whose progress through sub-zero conditions has been halted by an attack of three Chinese communist divisions in December 1950.

US marines with North Korean captives

Before the entry of the Chinese forces into the war, the US and UN forces appeared to have the stronger hand. Here, during the initial 1950 advance, US marines are guarding three recently captured North Koreans.

Parachute drop, Korea, 1951

Air power was a crucial part of the Korean campaign. The US Air Force was dominant at first, and was able to heavily disrupt North Korean supply lines and industrial capacity, to the extent that the Chinese were dependent on packhorses for their supplies. However the introduction of Russian-manufactured MiG-15s piloted by Russians evened up the battle, as these planes were able to outmanoeuvre B-29 bombers and the fighters that flew with them. It was only the introduction of F-86 Sabres on the US side that allowed them to regain air dominance.

In a war that became bogged down on or around the 38th parallel from 1951 to 1953, the ability to use air power and cover to jump territory was decisive. This massive parachute drop, covered by air by US forces was one of many steps forward taken by UN troops.

US marines capture Chinese soldiers

Marines of the 1st Division capture Chinese communist soldiers on the central Korean front at Hoengsong. After the 1950–51 winter's reverses, US forces fought their way back north under the field command of General Ridgway. By 2 March 1951 when this picture was taken, they were back in the region of the 38th parallel, the border that had divided North and South Korea before the North's invasion.

US soldiers, Korea

In the early stages of the Korean War, a grief-stricken American infantryman, whose friend has been killed in action, is comforted by another soldier, 28 August 1950.

Burnt out Russian tanks in Budapest

During the revolt in Hungary in 1956, burnt out Russian T34 tanks lie in a street in Budapest following a battle. When Soviet troops crushed the rebellion, somewhere between 25,000 and 50,000 Hungarian rebels were killed as well as 7,000 Soviet troops. Thousands more were wounded, and hundreds of thousands left the country as refugees. The Left in the Western bloc had been largely tolerant of the Russian regime but the brutal Soviet intervention in Hungary disillusioned many, making it clear that the repressive nature of the Soviet bloc was not about to change in spite of Khrushchev's apparent move away from extreme Stalinism.

Soviet base in Havana, Cuban Missile Crisis

A view of a Soviet military base in the harbour area of Havana in August 1962. As the Cold War continued, this was probably the closest the world came to actual nuclear conflict between the superpowers. Since the failed Bay of Pigs invasion in 1961, Castro had feared another US invasion, so he agreed to a Soviet plan to install missile on the island. Photographs such as this one showed an increased military presence, but on 22 October 1962 President Kennedy announced the discovery (made a week earlier via surveillance photographs) of Soviet nuclear weapons in Cuba.

A week of terrifying brinkmanship ensued as Kennedy demanded the removal of the weapons. At one point Khrushchev demanded that the US withdraw their weapons from Turkey in exchange, but eventually the two nations backed away from war – the Soviets withdrew their weapons in the expectation of assurances that the USA would not invade Cuba.

US soldiers in Vietnam

One major problem encountered by US soldiers in the Vietnam War was the difficulty of the terrain in which they had to fight. This photograph of US troops provides a glimpse of the difficulties faced in dealing with the jungle – the major problem being the difficulty of getting around, and the endless opportunities for ambush provided to an enemy who knew the land. The increased use of napalm as the war continued was largely based on the difficulty of negotiating the jungle, but it was also a weapon that was indiscriminate in its destruction.

US soldiers with machine gun, Vietnam

This image shows US soldiers in the American assault on Hill 881 in 1967. Hills 861, 881 North, and 881 South lay to the north-west of the Khe Sanh Combat Base and were the scene of the well-known "Hill Fights". General Westmoreland hoped to hold the Khe Sanh area because he aimed to engage the North Vietnamese forces in a battle that would draw them into a decisive defeat. The General was convinced that the enemy was trying to use the same strategies they had used to defeat the French in 1954 at Dien Bien Phu, and persisted in his own strategy as a result. As a result there was a strange sequence of events whereby the hills would be taken and cleared, then abandoned by US forces, only to be retaken once again by force. The Marines also suffered from problems with their equipment, in particular the newly issued M-16 rifle which was prone to jamming. Over 600 US servicemen died or were injured in the Hill Fights, which General Victor Krulak called "the toughest fight we had in Vietnam". This chain of events led on to the infamous January–April 1968 siege of Khe Sanh, which lasted seventy-seven days. Khe Sanh was eventually retained, but was subsequently abandoned by US troops as the focus of the war shifted. The 1968 Tet Offensive had substantially changed the strategic situation in the war and Khe Sanh was no longer as crucial as it had once seemed.

Vietnamese soldier firing

During the battle for Hill 881, a Vietnamese soldier fires his weapon. The South Vietnamese forces would later become a key part of Nixon's plan to finish the war through "Vietnamization"which aimed to transfer more of the burden. To increase the size of the ARVN all South Vietnamese men between the ages of seventeen and 43 were to be called up. However it became clear that withdrawing US troops under these cirumstances would lead to the defeat of the South and the focus switched to other means of ending the war.

Assault on Hill 881

A US soldier with a fallen comrade during the assault on Hill 881.

A US soldier beats a Viet Cong captive

In 1966, a US soldier hits a captured Viet Cong fighter in a river. The US side of the Vietnam War was widely and freely covered by journalists and photographers, and many of the images that came back were uncomfortable for the public at home and helped slowly to turn public opinion against the war. In the early stages of the war there was widespread support and respect for the bravery and suffering of the troops, but as this started to change the mood of the country and its attitude to the war slowly changed too. Many US soldiers felt let down by this change of public opinon as, for them, the battle continued unabated.

US troops in a Vietnamese village

A US patrol searches a Vietnamese village. It was hard to fight an enemy that instead of being made up of regular troops was based largely in and around the peasant villages of the countryside. There were Viet Cong sympathisers in both the North and South of the country. Between 1968 and 1971 the Nixon government attempted to track down and assassinate NLF sympathisers by using infiltrated informers.

My Lai, Vietnam

In March 2001 Lawrence Colburn and Hugh Thompson returned to the village of My Lai to dedicate a peace park and school in the village where they had once, as US soldiers, helped to rescue a few civilians from the notorious My Lai massacre. In doing so they had had to ignore orders from a superior officer and to pull their guns on colleagues whose actions they could not condone. There were other brave men on the American side – Ronald Ridenhour who was brave enough to expose the events of the massacre to the media and Congress, and those troops who refused to follow orders by killing defenceless Vietnamese. But this was a terrible moment in the history of the war and, whether or not it was an exceptional incident, it was one that finally helped to convince the public that what was happening in Vietnam was wrong.

US surgical unit in Vietnam

Medical conditions in wartime are inevitably difficult. This photograph shows a US soldier being treated at a US camp in the Vietnam War in 1971. Far from the clean and well-lit conditions of hospitals, a military tent provides a makeshift operating theatre.

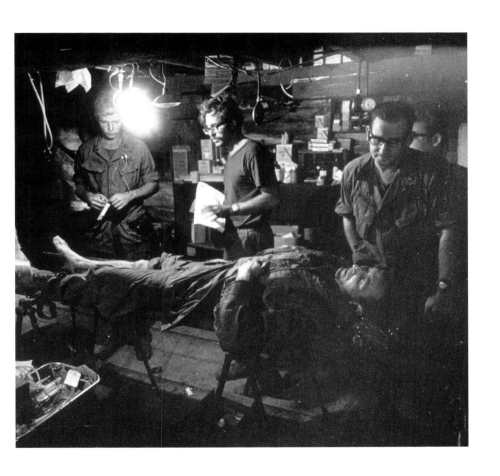

US warplanes over Vietnam

In an attempt to counteract the difficulties of jungle warfare in Vietnam, the Americans resorted to the use of various unconventional techniques. As well as using the incendiary napalm, they used twenty million gallons of herbicide between 1962 and 1971 in an attempt to remove foliage which provided cover for enemy forces. The intention was also to deprive the enemy forces of food and supplies. Herbicides used included Agent Purple, Agent White, Agent Pink and Agent Orange (the colours referred to the containers of the agents rather than to their physical appearance). Agent Orange's long term legacy of health problems is ongoing for veterans of the war on both sides and their descendants. These effects include cancers, Hodgkins disease, deformities, diabetes and spina bifida, all of which have been caused by exposure to the chemicals.

Czech civilians with Russian tank

The 1968 Prague Spring, in which Czech leader Alexander Dubcek attempted to reform communism in his country was, like the 1956 Hungary uprising, crushed by Soviet intervention. In this picture crowds of Czechs attempt to face down and reason with the Russian tank commanders who are taking over the city.

Czech civilians climb on Russian tank

The Soviets reimposed their power by force of numbers rather than by use of crushing force. The Czechs here climbing on the Russian tank are showing brave defiance – dozens were killed by Russian troops in the aftermath of the engagement and many others were injured. As with Hungary in 1956, the West took no action. To do so would have been risky in the atmosphere of nuclear threat, and in any case in 1968 the Americans were involved in both an election and the Vietnam War. The Soviets were apparently prepared to invade even if this did provoke a confrontation with the West. Czech leader Alexander Dubcek finally returned to Prague in 1989 after the collapse of the communist regime, as part of the first administration of the "Velvet Revolution".

PART FIVE

WIND OF CHANGE

*The post-war disintegration of empire –
decolonisation in Africa and the Far East – conflict in
the Third World – local nationalisms and uprisings*

British counterinsurgency patrol
in Malaya, 1959

Two British soldier take a break on a counterinsurgency patrol in the
Malayan jungle in 1959, their expressions illustrating the truth of Lawrence
of Arabia's dictum that battling a rebellion is like "learning to eat soup with
a knife". Though most members of their 9,000-strong enemy, the Malayan
Races' Liberation Army (MRLA) had been rooted out by 1958, the war
continued until 1960, having begun in 1948. Although Britain's
counterinsurgency operations in Malaya were, on the face of it, an
undeniable short-term success in that they enabled Britain to re-establish
order and withdraw from their colonial occupation, the battle for hearts and
minds that is supposed to have been such a large part of this success, was
more myth than reality. The scope and scale of most such projects was not
great and they were mainly implemented only in the closing stages of the
war. In reality, the campaign was brutal and riddled with abuses such as the
display of guerilla corpses and their decapitation; a photograph of a Royal
Marine commando holding up the heads of two insurgents, for example,
caused an outcry in 1952, with the British government noting privately that
"under international law a similar case in wartime would be a war crime".
During the war, nearly the entire Chinese population of 400,000 to
500,000 were forcibly resettled in around 400 heavily guarded, fenced
villages where they endured great hardship.

Anti-British riots, Egypt, 1952

This photograph, taken in the Egyptian town of Ismailia in January 1952, shows a British soldier, with a spare magazine at the ready, directing the fire of his companion's Bren gun. British troops had occupied a garrison in the Canal Zone since before the First World War, but there had always been resistance to this. In 1952, patrolling British troops had come under fire from Egyptian rebels and the resulting strong anti-British feeling in Cairo led to riots in which the exclusive Turf Club, Shepheard's Hotel and Barclays Bank, among other buildings, were burnt and looted. A number of British citizens, most of them members of the Turf Club, which was almost totally destroyed, were killed. In response to the killing of an Irish-born nun by Egyptian fighters who had forced their way into her convent, British troops seized control of the town of Ismailia, during which they killed forty Egyptian police officers. Soon after the Cairo riots King Farouk was overthrown by Neguib and Nasser and in 1954 Gamal Abdel Nasser became president. Two years later, to British and French outrage, he nationalized the Suez Canal which led to the 1956 Suez Crisis in which Britain, France and Israel allied themselves in an attack on Egypt.

Mau Mau Rebellion, Kenya

A British police inspector interrogates Kikuyu men suspected of being part of the Mau Mau Rebellion in 1952. Mau Mau was a militant African nationalist movement in Kenya during the 1950s; its aim was to overthrow British rule and force European settlers from the country. Supposedly, members, who were overwhelmingly Kikuyu, had to take an oath to this effect. In August 1952, the Kenyan government imposed a curfew in some districts on the outskirts of Nairobi where Mau Mau had allegedly been setting fire to the homes of Africans who had refused to take the Mau Mau oath. In October of the same year, Senior Chief Waruhui was assassinated for his outspoken opposition to Mau Mau and the British government announced that it would send troops to Kenya. As part of the resulting crackdown and the declaration of a State of Emergency, the future president of Kenya and leader of the Kenya African Union, Jomo Kenyatta, was arrested for alleged involvement in Mau Mau. In November, British forces responded to the declaration of open rebellion by Mau Mau by arresting 2,000 Kikuyus suspected of membership of the organization. The struggle continued until, by January 1956, the official death toll for Mau Mau activists killed by British forces in Kenya since 1952 stood at 10,173. Finally, following the election of Jomo Kenyatta as prime minister in the country's first non-racial elections and Kenyan independence in 1963, a general amnesty was announced for all Mau Mau activists. In December 1964, Kenya was declared a republic with Jomo Kenyatta as its first president.

Aden Emergency, 1963 – 67

One of five soldiers injured by a grenade thrown at troops of the Royal Northumberland Fusiliers in the labyrinthine streets of the Crater district as they moved to disperse a crowd of demonstrators during the Aden Emergency. In an attempt to prevent its Aden Protectorate from being swallowed up by North Yemen, Britain tried to unite the states of the region prior to granting independence. In 1963, Aden was incorporated into the Federation of Arab Emirates of the South which was soon renamed the Federation of South Arabia. This was not popular and resulted in a rebellion against British rule which came to be known as the Aden Emergency. It began with a grenade attack by the National Liberation Front (NLF) against the British High Commissioner in 1963 which killed one and injured fifty; in response a State of Emergency was declared. In 1964, Britain declared that it would grant independence in 1968, but mass riots in 1967 by the NLF and the rival Front for the Liberation of Occupied South Yemen (FLOSY) in the old Arab Quarter led to many attacks on troops; an Aden Airlines flight was also destroyed in mid-air at this time. Britain finally pulled out in 1967 leaving the Federation of South Arabia under NLF control. Aden subsequently became the capital of the People's Republic of South Yemen, renamed the People's Democratic Republic of Yemen in 1970. When northern and southern Yemen united in 1990, Sanaa became the capital of the new country.

A Biafran patrol enters a destroyed village, 1967

The Nigerian Civil War began in July 1967, the culmination of instability that had threatened the country since independence in 1960. The immediate cause of the war was the coup and counter-coup of 1966 which had a tremendously negative impact on relations between the major ethnic groups in the country. In an attempt to hold the country together the original four regions were divided into twelve states in May 1967. The former Eastern Region, under the leadership of Lieutenant Colonel Ojukwu reacted to this move by the central government without consultation by declaring the independent state of Biafra. The federal government in Lagos attempted to resolve this secession, which they regarded as illegal, peacefully, but without success. In an effort to avoid the disintegration of the country the central government resorted to force which they believed would bring about a quick resolution. By August 1967, however, the Biafran forces had extended to the war to the Mid-Western Region in an attempt to relieve pressure on the northern front and to threaten Lagos.

Biafran patrol, Nigerian Civil War

The Nigerian Civil War developed into a protracted and bloody struggle. At the end of April 1969, after two years, the Biafrans were still holding on, though to a drastically reduced area. Realizing that the end was near, Biafran leader Lieutenant Colonel Ojukwu and his immediate family fled the area in January 1970. His successor as commander of the Biafran Army surrendered to the federal government on 14 January 1970.

Celebrations following the coup in Portugal, 1974

In April 1974, General Antonio Spinola assumed power in Portugal by means of a coup which toppled the right-wing regime of Dr Caetano. The coup was mounted by young officers weary after thirteen years of colonial wars, largely in Mozambique and Angola, and was relatively bloodless – three people were reported dead and thirty-nine wounded.

The destruction of *HMS Sir Galahad*, Falklands War

HMS Sir Galahad was launched in 1966, designed to carry 340 troops, but capable of transporting up to 534. She could carry 340 tons of cargo – for example, sixteen tanks, thirty-four other vehicles, 120 tons of petrol and oil and thirty tons of ammunition. On 8 June 1982, during the Falklands War, *HMS Sir Galahad* was attacked together with *HMS Sir Tristram* by planes of the Argentine Air Force in Bluff Cove. She was hit by a number of bombs and very badly damaged. She had been attacked previously by Argentinian A-4B planes on 24 May while in San Carlos Water and hit by a 1000-pound bomb which fortunately did not explode. At the time of the attack in Bluff Cove she was involved in unloading soldiers of the 1st Welsh Guards and forty-eight of them were killed in explosions and the subsequent fires. Her hulk was later towed out to sea where it is now an official war grave.

A British paratrooper, Falklands War, 1982

In May 1982, having been ordered to seize Argentinian positions in the area of Goose Green, British paratroopers attacked with support from artillery and naval guns. In the intense battle which ensued, fought against a well dug in, numerically superior enemy over ground with very little natural cover, the paratroopers succeeded in taking the positions. There were many casualties, including the commanding officer, Lieutenant Colonel H. Jones, who was posthumously awarded a Victoria Cross.

Child soldier, Sierra Leone

Eleven-year-old Felix Musa pictured in Bo, Sierra Leone, with fellow child soldiers pressed to fight in the civil war. It is thought that up to 100,000 children in Africa were involved in armed conflict in 2004. Sierra Leone was notorious for its use of child soldiers in its ten-year-long civil war, when both the government and rebels recruited children. Felix was fighting on the side of the Kamajor militia. Before the war, the Mende word "kamajor" described a hunter brave enough to face wild animals in the forest and with magical powers. In response to growing numbers of government troops colluding with Revolutionary United Front rebels in looting villages, these village hunters recruited young men to militias where they were schooled in weapons handling, Kamajor history and the secrets believed to make them invulnerable to bullets.

An Indonesian soldier covers the body of journalist Sander Thoenes, East Timor

In September 1999, Dutch journalist Sander Thoenes travelled to Dili in East Timor to cover the landing of Interfet peace keepers. While it is not yet entirely certain who killed him and how or why, he and a motorbike rider Florindo were apparently attacked by Indonesian soldiers in uniform while they were travelling from the Turismo Hotel to Bekora. Sander Thoene's body was found dead in Bekora on the outskirts of Dili on the morning of 22 September 1999. He had been killed, most likely instantly, by a single bullet which had entered his back and passed through his heart and lungs.

PART SIX

THE MIDDLE EAST AND THE MODERN WORLD

Post-war strife in the Middle East – the birth of Islamic fundamentalism – the first Gulf War – 9/11 and the fall of the Taliban – the invasion of Iraq

King David Hotel Bomb, 22 July 1946

From the early 1800s onwards, there were a number of waves of Jewish immigration (Aliyah) to Palestine, largely influenced by the spread of Zionist ideas. From the late 1930s the Zionist group Irgun had been facilitating immigration of European Jews to the British Mandate of Palestine, partly as a haven from the pogroms of Europe and also as part of a strategy to entrench the Jewish settlement and to defend it against Arab hostility. The British authorities tried to restrict this immigration. The British Government had supported the idea of a Jewish national home, notably in the 1917 Balfour Declaration, but the 1939 White Paper effectively abandoned this idea in favor of restricted immigration. In 1944, under the leadership of future Israeli president Menachem Begin, Irgun undertook a new terrorist campaign against the British to weaken their resolve and to influence public opinion in Britain against the continued occupation of the territory.

The King David Hotel was the site of the British military command and the British Criminal Investigation Division. Irgun chose it as a target following British troops' invasion of the Jewish Agency on 29 June, 1946, during which they confiscated large quantities of documents. At about the same time, more than 2,500 Jews from all over Palestine were placed under arrest. The information about Jewish Agency operations, including intelligence activities in Arab countries, was taken to the King David Hotel. The bomb resulted in the deaths of 92 Britons, Arabs and Jews. It also temporarily led to a splintering of the Jewish Resistance Movement. Irgun continued to fight the British and were probably also responsible for the alleged massacre at Deir Yassin in the 1948 Arab-Israeli War. The group was formally dissolved and integrated into the Israeli Defence Forces in 1948, shortly after the proclamation of the state of Israel.

Israeli Army, 1947

In the post-war period various Jewish groups formed shifting alliances to fight against the British and the Arabs of the area as they attempted to defend themselves and establish a Jewish state. After the state of Israel came into being these informal groups were co-opted into the official Israeli Army. In this image, recruits of the fledgling Israeli Army are seen during a training exercise in 1947.

British paratroopers in Jordan

In 1922, following Arab anger at the Balfour declaration, the British formed the semi-autonomous, Arab Emirate of Transjordan in all Palestinian territory east of the Jordan river ruled by Hashemite Prince Abdullah and a British High Commisioner. The country became the independent Hashemite Kingdom of Transjordan in May 1946 after the British mandate ended. The country was renamed after it annexed the West Bank in 1950, although only the United Kingdom recognized this annexation. The country opposed the establishment of the state of Israel and participated in warfare between the new state and the surrounding Arab countries.

These British paratroopers are setting up a Bren gun position against the backdrop of the desert and local Arab observers. Following the 1951 assassination of Abdullah, sixteen-year-old Prince Hussein became king. In the early years of his reign he had to call on the British for military help as part of a special defence treaty between Jordan and Britain which lasted until 1957.

Six-Day War, 1967

A Syrian soldier lies dead on the road to Damascus, next to a Syrian armoured tank during the Arab-Israeli Six-Day War. This war was a pivotal event in the modern history of the Middle East. There had been a series of border incidents between Israel and its neighbours. On 5 June 1967, Israel launched a pre-emptive attack on the Egyptian Air Force after Egypt closed the Straits of Tiran to Israel's shipping, and deployed troops in the Sinai.

The subsequent, brief but decisive war involved Jordan and Syria as well as Egypt fighting against Israel. There are many theories and conjectures about specific events of the war that are hard to substantiate one way or another, but however it came about the war was a major defeat for the Arab states. It resulted in Israel controlling the Gaza Strip, the Golan Heights, the Sinai Peninsula and the West Bank, which would continue to be bitterly disputed areas for many years to come.

Arab-Israeli War, 1973

A group of Israeli soldiers pet an Alsatian dog left behind after fighting at the village of Jabta Al Chatab in the front line of Syrian action during the Arab-Israeli War of October 1973. The 1973 War, also known to the opposing sides as the Yom Kippur War and the Ramadan War, centered on the territories that Israel had annexed in the Six-Day War. There were heavy losses on both sides, but the end result was that Israel retained the disputed territory.

Lebanese Civil War

Lebanon was a microcosm of the problems of the Middle East, with enmities between various Muslim and Arab sects as well as a Christian minority that dated back to the colonial period. Following hostile exchanges between Palestinians and Phalangist groups, civil war broke out in 1975 and in spite of various ceasefires and pauses this lasted for nearly sixteen years in total, with both Syria and Israel becoming involved in supporting groups within the country. In this picture from January 1990, militiamen with AK-47 and RPG weapons talk tactics in a street in the city of Beirut. This was once a grand colonial city, but by 1990 it had largely been destroyed or reduced to rubble.

Al Aqsa Mosque 2000

Palestinians pray at the Al Aqsa Mosque in October 2000 after being denied entry by the Israeli Army. The mosque stands in Jerusalem on an ancient holy site for Muslims, known as Haram-al-Sharif (Noble Sanctuary) and lies opposite the Dome of the Rock on the Temple Mount, which is revered as a Jewish holy place. Inevitably, the mosque has been at the centre of a number of critical moments in the Israeli-Palestinian struggle.

In 1969 a fire was started there by Dennis Rohan, an Australian evangelical Christian who hoped to hasten the coming of the Messiah by his actions. Before he was found to be the culprit, riots broke out in Arab areas on the assumption that this was a direct attack by Israelis on the Muslim holy place.

In September 2000, Ariel Sharon made a remarkable visit to walk about Haram-al-Sharif, an event which was taken by Palestinians as a direct provocation. This led on to Muslim riots and to the "Al-Aqsa Intifada". Sharon's ensuing election as Prime Minister in 2001 was partly the result of Israeli voters' desire to elect a hardliner to deal with that Intifada.

Stone-throwing in Ramallah, 2000

On 16 October 2000, following the funeral of Raid Hamoudeh in Ramallah, violence broke out yet again as part of the ongoing Intifada. Hamoudeh had been shot and fatally wounded the previous day by the Israeli Army. Palestinian youths, disillusioned with the political process and with Yasser Arafat's failures to advance the peace process, responded in the now familiar way, with burning tyres and stone-throwing. This fighter is taking cover behind the burnt-out remains of cars to aim his slingshot. At least sixty-nine Palestinians died or were injured on this day by Israeli troops who responded to the provocation with a mixture of teargas, rubber bullets and sniper fire. Even as the fighting continued Yasser Arafat and Ehud Barak were meeting in the Egyptian resort of Sharm el-Sheikh to negotiate, but few on either side on the streets of Ramallah that day believed that any progress would be made in the near or even distant future.

Two young Afghanis with guns, 1987

These two boys from Afghanistan pose with their guns in 1987, during the war to eject the Russian occupiers. One can only guess at the brutalizing and desensitizing effects of the experience of war at such an early age. Covert Western support for the Mujaheddin who fought the Soviets in this conflict, including extensive arms supplies from the CIA, made a considerable difference to the outcome of the war. But the unforeseen long term effect of this support was to assist in training a generation of extremist Muslims in the art of war. Many fighters who went on to fight in other conflicts had their first battlefield experiences in Afghanistan, including Osama bin Laden and other high level members of Al Qaeda, as well as Mullah Omar and other prominent members of the Taliban. The religious schools set up in Afghanistan and across the border in Pakistan evolved into virtual training centers for Islamic radicals. The challenges of Islamic fundamentalism were not caused by the Afghanistan conflict, but the ways in which Islamic terrorism in the modern world has developed were certainly strongly influenced by this conflict.

Combat sequence, Gulf War 1991

These photographs are rare images of ground troops in action in 1991 in the desert during the action to liberate Kuwait following the Iraqi invasion. In this sequence, Mike Moore photographed Private Thomas Gow of the British Army as he lies in the sand facing enemy fire from a buried personnel carrier. Under fire, Gow jumps up and runs forward, across the mine-strewn no-man's-land. One can see bullets hitting the ground next to him. Crouching down, Gow throws a grenade and destroys the enemy vehicle allowing the advance to continue. Private Gow was awarded the Military Medal by the Queen for his bravery that morning.

Kurds crossing a footbridge in northern Iraq

The hidden victims of war are often the displaced populations who flee from war zones, leaving behind their homes and possessions to seek safety. During the 1990-1991 conflict many Kurds hoped for the overthrow of the Ba'athist regime. Following the ceasefire, some Kurds continued to rise up against the Iraqi regime but were met by helicopter gunships and troops of the defeated but angry Saddam Hussein.

US and European troops safeguarded Kurdish enclaves and tried to establish a Kurdish "safe haven" in the north of the country, but as the protection of the occupying troops was withdrawn, leaving only a lightly armed UN protection force, many Kurds fled, fearing the savagery of Saddam's reprisals. As recently as 1988 Saddam had led a campaign in which as many as 100,000 Kurds died, including the 5,000 gassed in Halabja. As many as 1.3 million Kurdish refugees escaped to Iran and 450,000 fled across the icy mountains to Turkey, crossing rope bridges and treacherous mountain terrain on the way.

US soldier in Kuwait with night sight

After the 1990 - 1991 combat in Iraq, the UN and coalition forces entered into a period of containment of the Iraq regime. Alongside sanctions and no-fly zones within Iraq, a military presence was maintained beyond Iraq's borders. The remaining presence of US troops in the region was a source of grievance in the Arab world, although the Saddam Hussein regime was widely recognized to be a danger to its neighbours.

This image shows an American soldier looking through a night-vision scope and holding a grenade-style launcher while stationed in Kuwait in 1997 as part of the coalition forces left to protect Kuwait's borders.

Attack on the World Trade Center

The world changed on the morning of 11 September 2001. The images are so familiar that it is occasionally hard to recall the shock that such a devastating attack was taking place on American soil, and was being broadcast around the world in real time. This picture was taken across the Hudson River, from Hoboken, shortly after the towers collapsed. Lower Manhattan lies under a pall of smoke and dust thrown up into the sky. As thousands fled across the Brooklyn Bridge, or up Manhattan's Avenues towards the relative safety of midtown, the aftermath of the worst suicide attack in history lay behind them. Myriad images and film sequences of the impacts, of the fires and of the terrible fall of the towers were broadcast immediately around the world. A terrorist attack that provoked a "war on terror", this led on to the military action in Afghanistan and Iraq. It also caused a profound change in the relationship between the USA and the rest of the world, a change that is still developing.

Northern Alliance fighter, Afghanistan

A foot-soldier of the Northern Alliance holding an AK-47 rifle on the front line at Gazestan. Shortly after the attack on the World Trade Center towers in September 2001, the US initiated an invasion of Afghanistan to dislodge the extremist Taliban government, which was believed to be sheltering training camps for Al Qaeda. Afghanistan had suffered from years of warfare, going back to the Russian invasion and beyond. After the mujaheddin, helped by the west, drove the Russians out, the country was to a large degree lawless, with local tribal loyalties holding sway over centralized law.

The Taliban came to power in 1994, ruling approximately two thirds of the territory with their extremist, neo-medieval take on Islam. The Northern Alliance were the most powerful group in the North of the country and it was to them that the US turned in seeking allies for the attack on the Taliban. There were heavy clashes between the two sides in the North of the country before the fall of Kabul spelt the end of the Taliban.

Afghan woman with gun

An Afghan woman, "Umera" aged 23, poses with a gun in the lead-up to the invasion of Afghanistan. The message is that she is ready to take up arms against the Taliban in the event of war. To openly wear makeup, lipstick and nail varnish, under the repressive Taliban regime meant instant punishment. As well as insisting on absolute compliance with their interpretation of Islamic rules, they banned music and dancing, insisted that all men grow beards and made kite-flying illegal. On 14 November 2001, after the overthrow of the Taliban, The Guardian newspaper in the UK reported that men were rushing out to buy razors to shave their hated beards, and in the streets and open spaces of Kabul, children everywhere were flying kites.

Blowing up caves in Afghanistan

The Afghan mountains have defeated many invaders including the troops of the British Empire who failed to pacify the country and, eventually, the Soviets. The harsh environment, dangerous passes and mountain slopes and networks of caves make for a defensible natural landscape, well known to locals, but dangerous for outsiders.

After the fall of the Taliban it was widely believed that Osama Bin Laden had fled to a cave network in the mountains that border Pakistan. British troops are here seen detonating charges to try to clear insurgent forces believed to be hiding out in mountain caves. Shortly after this image was captured, the US detonated two 2,000-pound (907-kg) "thermobaric" bombs. These massive explosive devices send suffocating blasts through cave complexes, and were aimed at mountain caves where enemy fighters were believed to be hiding. In spite of these efforts Bin Laden apparently escaped from the allied forces and was later believed to be in hiding across the border in Pakistan.

Direct hit on Saddam Hussein's palace, Second Gulf War

The First Gulf War in 1991 had ended with coalition forces pulling back after the liberation of Kuwait, rather than fighting on to support the Iraqi uprising against Saddam Hussein. As a result, and in spite of the extensive sanctions employed against the regime, Saddam survived as ruler until the second Gulf War in 2003.

The 2003 invasion was justified by reference to the weapons of mass destruction that Saddam was believed by many to be holding. He had shown himself capable of using such weapons when he gassed the Kurds in the Iraq-Iran war, and there was some genuine confusion as to what reserves he still held. But few were in doubt that the real aim of this invasion was regime change, specifically the removal of Saddam. His extravagant presidential palaces were targeted both because they were used as offices by the Ba'ath party and presidential guard, and because of their military capacities. But beyond that they held great significance both for the Iraqis and the invaders, and images such as this one, of a direct hit on Saddam's riverside Presidential Palace in central Baghdad, carried a clear message.

Iraqis search for downed Allied pilot, Second Gulf War

In a city under siege, rumours and hysteria take hold easily. In March 2003 as allied forces fought their way towards Baghdad, this crowd gathered on the banks of the River Tigris in the belief that a British pilot had landed in the river after his plane was downed. A mixture of lynch-mob mentality and rubberneck fascination with the unknown attackers was displayed as the crowd feverishly searched the banks of the river, even at one stage setting fire to the reeds in an attempt to smoke the missing pilot out. Other captured pilots and troops were killed or beaten by Iraqi troops in this period – the first images of captured US troops were broadcast on the same day as this incident. Western journalists covering the incident, and viewers at home watched with trepidation, fearing the worst if the pilot were captured.

A Gurkha stops Iraqis on the road to Basra, Second Gulf War

In April 2003 during the Iraq War, a Gurkha of the British Army commands four Iraqi men out of a vehicle west of Basra. Two Puma helicopters were sent out to intercept the vehicle with four Iraqi men on board, and the men were later taken off for questioning.

The roads of Iraq following the invasion were a treacherous and dangerous place. The use of suicide bombing increased markedly as the insurgency continued, but from the start of the invasion allied troops were in danger as they patrolled. Roadside bombs, many of them very sophisticated, were used to ambush vehicles. And approaching vehicles were suspect until they proved harmless. Iraqis are accustomed to driving at high speed on the desert highways, but the soldiers on roadblocks set up to check on passing vehicles were inevitably nervous of approaching cars – this is reflected in the caution shown by the pictured Gurkha.

British troops airlifted into Basra, Second Gulf War

The US strategy for the Second Gulf War in 2003 was to take the country as fast as possible by heading straight for Baghdad. The operation started with extensive bombing, followed by a massive troop deployment and after the March invasion, US troops were on the outskirts of Baghdad within weeks. Arguments would continue as to whether or not this was the right strategy. It allowed for a quick invasion, with a relatively small number of troops, but by failing to secure parts of the country as they proceeded to Baghdad it can be argued that this policy allowed many of the future insurgents to melt away from Baghdad to local power bases.

The British who, along with the Australians, were the other main participants in the coalition forces, were charged with pacifying the south of the country around the city of Basra. Here British Marines from 40 Commando are inserted into Basra by TRAF helicopters as British forces enter the city. The political difficulties faced by the Blair government in getting into the war were perhaps reflected in the fact that the British were asked to occupy a part of the country that was relatively sympathetic to the invasion. Basra is a largely Shia town, and had suffered at the hands of Saddam in the past. The British were able to at least attempt to win the hearts and minds of the locals, patrolling at times on foot and without helmets to project a more approachable image.

A statue of Saddam Hussein stands in front of his son Uday's blazing office, Second Gulf War

As American marines occupied positions in eastern Baghdad on this day in April 2003, the city was under attack from the air as well as on land. Saddam's palaces had been particular targets of the bombing campaign. Their symbolic importance was great, and while Iraqi opinion was divided on the campaign, Saddam Hussein and his family were widely hated. The partially staged destruction of Saddam's statue which marked the closing stages of the Battle for Baghdad seemed at the time to represent the defeat of the Ba'ath Party and its dictatorial dominance of the country.

Saddam's sons Uday and Qusay were vicious thugs, hated by those who they had repressed. This picture shows Uday's office, which was also extensively looted, in flames as his father's statue stands in front. When American troops cornered and killed the two brothers in July, they issued macabre pictures of their corpses. This caused some outrage in the Arab world in particular. The US justification was that the pictures needed to be shown as proof that the sons were dead, and to convince the Iraqi populace that the regime really was finished, not just in hiding and awaiting their chance to return.

The display of dead trophy prisoners, and the use of execution videos became a major part of the insurgency. In the age of the internet, a video or image, no matter how gruesome, can be transmitted around the world in seconds. Where early wars had been recorded in photographs and first person accounts by war correspondents, images have now become a part of the process, a weapon to be used as propaganda and as an event in themselves.

Fallujah shootings

When Iraq was invaded, some areas were harder to pacify than others. The town of Al Fallujah, approximately fifty kilometers north-west of Baghdad is a Sunni Muslim desert town, and from the start feelings ran high against the invasion. In the later stages of the invasion in April 2003, US troops were using the local school as a base. A demonstration against their presence turned to tragedy, although as ever there were different accounts of the exact chain of events. The protestors held placards including at least a few in support of Saddam, stones were thrown, and according to the US spokesman, shots were fired from the crowd, or perhaps from houses behind the crowd. Either way, it is clear that the US forces, feeling that they were under threat, opened fire. The death toll was estimated by contemporary sources at thirteen, and many were hurt in the panic and stampede to escape the gunfire – in this picture some protestors duck for cover as others run away. This was one of two similar massacres in a three-day period.

Fallujah continued to be a serious thorn in the side of the Allied forces. A year later four US contractors were killed, mutilated and hung from a bridge there. In April 2004, 60,000 residents of the town fled from the siege mounted by US troops, as they combed the city trying to flush our insurgents. As many as a thousand people may have died in this operation. The town was partially destroyed, but in spite of the severity of the operation, the violence continued in the area, as insurgents from inside and outside Iraq continued to stoke hatred between Sunni and Shia and to oppose the Allies and their attempts to introduce democracy.

Dead Iraqi in front of the the palace gates, Second Gulf War

The 2003 invasion of Iraq was characterized by the active parties' endeavours to control public perception and information. In the lead-up to the invasion, the world's media showed footage of the "shock and awe" bombing raids, and journalists were embedded with allied troops. The invasion was largely covered by such embedded reporters, while the media inside Iraq were obliged to mention that their reports had been made via the censorship of government restrictions.

The invasion was launched on 20 March by predominantly American and British forces. Just two-and-a-half weeks later, Baghdad had been reached. There had been differing predictions before the invasion – on the one hand that Baghdad would be a quagmire of house-to-house combat, and on the other hand that the Iraqis would meet the allies with garlands once they knew Saddam was finished. Neither guess proved accurate. By 9 April much of the Ba'ath Party government had fled into hiding and there was fierce but sporadic resistance from the remnants of the Iraqi forces. Even as Mohammed Saeed al-Sahaf, Iraq's Information Minister, was bizarrely declaring to the world's media that the Iraqis were winning the battle, the pictures told a different story. Here, in the bloody aftermath of the battle for Baghdad, an Iraqi fighter's body, with his RPG at his feet, lies in front of the main palace gates. On television one could see pictures of American troops at the main airport at the same time as hearing the Iraqi Information Minister's claims that Iraqi troops had retaken the site.

On 1 May George W. Bush declared the end of combat operations in the belief that the war was effectively over. Saddam was gone, soon to be captured. But the long and brutal insurgency that followed made the short war for military control seem like only the prelude to a longer, more treacherous struggle.

WARNER BROS.
STUDIO TOUR
LONDON

THE MAKING OF
Harry Potter

Warner Bros. Studio Tour London

Family Ticket £20.75

Valid 24/08/2012 between ██:██ and 19:00

Enjoy your visit to the Warner ████ ██████ ███ Tour
Eaten your ticket marked at last ████████.co.uk secrets
for exclusive content and fantastic prizes

Includes VAT at the applicable rate.

Node 64
Tran 192012
Serial 330030

Order No 225765
Printed 3/07/2012
User 103

1000306432891992273

The images within the book have been selected principally from the archives of Mirrorpix, a unique resource drawing on the collections not just of the world famous Daily Mirror newspaper but also those of sister titles the Daily Herald, Sunday Mirror, The People, the Daily Record and Sunday Mail. The Daily Mirror was first published in 1903 as a journal for women. After initial success, sales declined and the owner, Alfred Harmsworth, took the bold decision to print photographs as an additional means of conveying the news. With this innovation the age of photojournalism was born and the new illustrated pictorial Daily Mirror became the first newspaper in the world to publish photography. The Daily Record and the Daily Herald were also of early foundation, established in 1895 and 1912 respectively and both making extensive use of photography once the Mirror had shown the way. For every picture that was printed in the newspaper at the time, the archive contains many that weren't and consequently a number of photographs are published here for the first time.